EMDR With Complex Trauma

Thomas Zimmerman, Ms.Ed., LPCC

EMDR Training Collaborative/EMDR Cleveland

Cover Artwork by Carol Anna McBride.

Medical Disclaimer: The following information is intended for licensed mental health therapists. Therapists should evaluate if the information presented in this book is appropriate for your unique and individual client. All information presented should be used at the reader's discretion and is their sole responsibility.

Copyright © 2024 by Thomas Zimmerman.

ISBN: 979-8-9917824-0-1

Reviews

"In *EMDR for Complex Trauma*, Tom acts as an encouraging and steady field guide to new (and experienced) EMDR therapists who encounter complicated, but common challenges in therapy. He brings a down-to-earth, approachable tone, generously sharing his accumulated wisdom from years of on-the-ground experience working with complex trauma as both a therapist, a consultant, and a trainer. As I read this I found myself imagining being in conversation with Tom through the mud of the common problems he described with my own clients. I have no doubt that this book will help thousands of newly trained EMDR therapists to find their way through discouragement, frustration, and confoundment to be able to appreciate not only the challenge, but the beauty and nuance of therapeutic work using EMDR with complex trauma." -April Griffin, MSW RSW RCC

"I wish this book existed when I was first trained as an EMDR therapist. However, I am grateful that it exists now as I embark on my journey as a consultant in training as I will utilize the invaluable information within to help support my consultees through the difficult work of treating C-PTSD using EMDR therapy." -Amy Larmon, LCSW-R, Certified EMDR Therapist and Consultant-in-Training

"This book puts into clear words the experiences I have seen over the eight years I've been doing EMDR. It speaks to trainers, like myself, and to new EMDR clinicians alike. Tom's writing eloquently speaks to the experience of EMDR and names the why of what happens when 'EMDR doesn't work' or a client 'isn't ready for EMDR.' This book superbly describes how to use all eight phases of standard protocol with fidelity in a way that builds confidence in the therapist and brings ease for the client. This book is the clinical internship of 500 hours we all wish we could have had after basic training. It is a MUST READ for all clinicians who use EMDR in their practice." -Leslie Pertz, LMSW, PMH-C, NIC

"I really can't begin to tell you how much I love this book. It is like a comforting warm coat on a cold frosty day, wrapped around you to stave off the chill. I just love every part, the exercises, scripts, examples, explanations--it is quite simply going to be my go-to book with EMDR work and, what's more, I know clients will find it a huge help too."
-Rebekah Jones, Consultant Psychotherapist, Certified EMDR Therapist

"*EMDR with Complex Trauma* by Thomas Zimmerman is an essential guide for clinicians, especially new EMDR therapists navigating the complexities of trauma work. Zimmerman offers practical strategies to address deep-seated emotional wounds while empowering therapists to trust their own therapeutic instincts. As a new clinician, I found this book invaluable in breaking the stigma around being an 'experiential' therapist—encouraging creative, adaptive approaches grounded in EMDR principles. From somatic interventions to the ethics of trauma treatment, Zimmerman demystifies the process and provides actionable insights, making this book both a manual and a thoughtful meditation on healing. A must-read for any therapist committed to transformative trauma care." -Naila Brown, MA, LPC-Associate, NCC

"This book is as insightful as it is reassuring and presented in a structure and format that make it easy to digest and refer back to. I particularly appreciated the brief, vulnerable moments of self-disclosure that welcomed me into your journey of self-discovery and professional learning and made me feel like it's okay to feel unsure from time to time. I'm sure this book will be a welcome addition to many EMDR therapists' libraries."
-Lionel Walters, Trauma Counsellor and Trainer

"I recently audited Part II of a foundational training where, in real-time, therapists were sharing their experience of hitting roadblocks while starting reprocessing, and all of the cases seemed to be complex trauma. All I can think is that, after the foundational manual, this book should be the next required reading. It breaks down treating our most complex clients in a manageable and understandable way. It is a perfect balance of understanding the "why" behind modifications made and practical applications and scripts to use with clients. In contrast to other books about complex trauma, this book is easy to read and digest. It is a "must have" on the shelf of every EMDR clinician." -Lisa Johanns, LPC

"An essential companion for the EMDR therapist. This book provides insights on needed considerations and adjustments in working with complex trauma. It serves as a guide map of sorts, offering direction when feeling stuck or questioning which direction to take with a client. It validates adaptations to the basic protocol, offers scripts for resourcing, and important cautious approaches for compassionate successful work in this area." -Rebecca Carr, NCC, LPC, PMH-C

"*EMDR with Complex Trauma* fills an important gap in the literature available to newer EMDR-trained therapists like me. No matter how well we're taught the standard protocol, even including some time devoted to adaptations for complex trauma and dissociation if we're lucky, basic training just doesn't give us enough preparation for treating most of the clients we're likely to meet. Other texts addressing treatment of complex trauma with EMDR exist, and some are excellent (if dense), but Zimmerman's book accomplishes what these others don't: it is clear, brief, easy to read, and gives a set of practical tools to break down the process in ways that both therapists and clients can understand. Zimmerman draws on years of experience as an EMDR clinician and personal experiences related to his own healing process, both of which make him uniquely qualified to write this book. I found the entire reading experience profoundly relatable and enlightening as someone who uses EMDR with neurodivergent clients with complex trauma histories. The 'dip your toe in' resources have been especially helpful, and I also appreciate having new language to simply and concretely describe the process of EMDR to clients who ask me questions like "what does 'go with that' even mean?" I have highlighting and underlining on almost every page, and I know this will be a book I refer to again and again. If you're an EMDR therapist, especially a newly trained one confused and overwhelmed by all the literature available to you, please do yourself and your clients a favor and add this book to your library!" -Maija Salins, LMSW, LMT, CST-D, SEP

"This manual is a true work of personal art. It is filled with lived experience and story, allowing readers to relate and understand the 'why and how' to approach complex trauma from an EMDR perspective. The metaphors and resources take complex clinical knowledge and translate it into simple and practical ways which promotes clinicians' confidence and creativity. I would recommend this skillfully crafted "manual" to any therapist." -Rhea Eady, RSW & MSW

Review credits: Helpful feedback on drafts of this book was received by April Griffin, MSW RSW RCC; Celine Polilli, MA, LPC; and Meg Kapil, PhD, CCS, RCC-ACS, in addition to the above reviewers.

Preface

I have written the book that I needed to write. It is the book that I would have needed to read when I was starting my EMDR journey with severely complex clients. I have looked closely at every word to help make sure that none are more complicated than I need them to be. I view this book as one part guide and one part meditation. My hope is that this perspective is helpful. It comes from a deep interest and passion in doing this work. There is beauty in the work we do. I hope that some of this beauty is communicated in these words. But more than anything, I hope that this book finds its way to you on a random Thursday and reminds you that the work you do is essential, that this work is almost always hard, that you already embody a lot of what your clients most need of you, and that difficulties in this work often contain the important gift of information about your client's unique and complex nervous system.

This is a different kind of book. It captures how one person does and understands EMDR therapy. It is not meant to be dogma but offered to expand possibility and flexibility when working with clients with severe trauma.

While I encourage you to purchase print copies of this book and share them with new trainees, much of its content is available at the website below. Because parts of this book may be shared separately, you will see that some of the guidance, examples, or metaphors repeat across multiple chapters.

https://EMDRwithComplexTrauma.com

Table of Contents

Before We Start
1. How Have We Tried to Heal from Complex Trauma? — 2
2. What if We've Been Overthinking It? — 5
3. The Ethics of Not Treating Trauma — 9
4. The Boat and the Whale Metaphor — 11
5. EMDR Is Not a Magic Wand — 14
6. No Part of This Is Easy — 16
7. Therapist Anxiety — 17
8. What Makes Complex Trauma So Complex for EMDR Therapy — 18
9. All the Hats You Wear — 20
10. How We Train You — 21

Phase One
11. Doing a Sensible Phase One — 24
12. How Exactly Should We Do Phase One? — 30

Phase Two
13. Phase Two Isn't Just Mindfulness Resources — 32
14. The Utility of Parts Work — 41
15. "Mindfulness Doesn't Work for Me:" Teaching It Differently — 45
16. Why Attachment Resources are Often Needed — 53
17. The Attachment Figure Resource Script — 56
18. Introducing Fire Extinguisher Resources Early — 65
19. Dip Your Toe In Sensory Grounding — 68
20. Dip Your Toe In For Flashbacks Script — 70
21. Dip Your Toe In Body Scan Script — 72
22. Dip Your Toe In Calm Scene Script — 74
23. Dip Your Toe In Blue Smoke Breathing Script — 76
24. Dip Your Toe In Hand Breathing Script — 78
25. Dip Your Toe In Attachment Figure Resource — 79
26. More About Consent From Parts — 80
27. Where the Standard EMDR Resources Tend to Go Bad and How to Fix Them — 81
28. The Utility of Containment — 85
29. "And Then the Client Dissociated" — 89

30. Blocking Beliefs Are Also Phase Two Problems	93
31. What Does Prepared Enough Mean?	100

Phases Three-Seven

32. The Utility of Informed Consent	105
33. Helping Clients Understand Their Role in this Dance	107
34. There is Nothing to Figure Out Today	111
35. Oh My, Where Do We Start?	113
36. The Canaries in the Coal Mine	122
37. Why Overactivation is a Problem in EMDR Therapy	125
38. The Videotape Approach	127
39. The Videotape Approach Script	131
40. When to Let Memories In, When to Container	135
41. Where Clients Get Stuck and How to Intervene	140
42. The Quicksand of Attachment Wound Targets	151
43. Understanding the Developmental Deficits of Attachment Wounds	153
44. Why Finishing Things Matters in EMDR Therapy	156
45. EMDR Therapy and Grief	158
46. Additional Strategies for Working with Absences in Memory	161
47. Trouble Finding an Individual Memory when Trauma was Daily	166

Phase Eight

48. The Elegance of the Future Prong	170
49. What Healing Doesn't Give You	172

Short Answers to Common Consult Questions

50. Initial Topics	174
51. Phase One Topics	180
52. Phase Two Topics	181
53. Phases Three-Seven Topics	182
54. Phase Eight Topics	191

Metaphor Index

Boat and the Whale (EMDR therapy requires the presence of enough adaptive information), 11-13, 26, 42, 56-57, 98, 100, 103, 115, 128, 135, 145, 152, 186

Brownie Mix (EMDR therapy consists of several simple ingredients; don't add extra stuff), 109, 144

Canaries in the Coal Mine (early-warning indicators that your plan may not go well), 122-126

Cinderblock on the Gas Pedal (pervasively traumatized nervous systems work differently), 50

Green Sign on the Highway (we notice our way to adaptive information, rather than create it on purpose), 112

Grill in the Backyard (not everything that wants to come should come), 137-138

Leaving the Barn Door Open (sometimes we need a door or a gate on the memory channel), 108, 128

Magic Wand (EMDR is not a magic wand, and you are not a magician), 11, 14-15

Marathon (trying to run a marathon today is a bad idea), 118

Mount Everest (you cannot metabolize a trauma the size of Mount Everest into adaptive information the size of a walnut), 53, 118-120, 185

Putting a Fence Around a Memory (as a way to prevent overactivation in processing phases), 136

Tricycle (like the three wheels of the tricycle, EMDR therapy has three core tasks), 14-15, 18, 38, 90, 109, 126, 186

Tunnel from France to England (you don't dig a tunnel under the English Channel and stop two miles short), 157

Video Game (we don't run past treasure in a video game; we need those assets to eventually overcome it), 157

Before We Start

The Uses of Sorrow

(In my sleep I dreamed this poem)

Someone I loved once gave me
a box full of darkness.

It took me years to understand
that this, too, was a gift.

--Mary Oliver

"The Uses of Sorrow" by Mary Oliver Reprinted by the permission of The Charlotte Sheedy Literary Agency as agent for the author. Copyright © 2006 by Mary Oliver with permission of Bill Reichblum

Chapter 1
How Have We Tried to Heal From Complex Trauma?

When I was a young child, I looked around my world and realized that the adults were not okay. They clearly didn't know what they were doing. They were saturated with their lives, their misadventures in love, and their moods. They were not functional enough to have the capacity to be of much real assistance to me. Work for them was exhausting and numbing. This was the mid-1970s, and it felt as though everyone had just survived something horrible. There was a backstory that a six-year-old couldn't quite understand but could feel its full sad weight pressing against him. Children were not the irreplaceable things that they have become. We were things that happened to you. Then, more of us were born as though springing straight out of their disillusionment and resentment in each other.

I realized young that I had to figure things out largely by myself. So I figured out how to survive. I learned quickly that the only thing worse than being ignored was being noticed. When I could very little measure of safety at home, in the community, or at school, I figured out how to disappear. I learned how to smile and to pretend that I was okay. When I could not connect, I learned how to feign connection. I learned to ride a bike in a city faster than anyone could catch me. Eventually, I learned that I could be smart. I could disconnect from my body and pain. Later, I came to Catholic mysticism and discovered that I could make a spirituality of self-erasure. I found community support and spiritual endorsement for my earliest survival strategies. I made a practice of disappearing nearly everything that made me human. I learned to master my teenage body and will. I told myself when I was hungry and when I would sleep. I chose to sleep on hard surfaces for the lesson of it. I did worse to rid myself of self. I did not need the church to remind me that bodies were bad. But it was nice to have a formal blessing and an altar thousands of years old for those central ideals. In some ways, everything worked remarkably well. Until it didn't. When I was 21 my mystical spirituality collapsed, and I fell unexpectedly into a fully male body with decidedly human emotions. I felt huge things moving and pressing around inside of me, not one of which I could name or tolerate. It took a long time for things to settle. It took decades longer for the actual work of healing to start.

Healing from complex trauma will be my life's work. It is the onion I will endlessly peel, and I will probably never find the little green sprig in its center. I have had the fortune to do great healing work. Much of what I learned from my recovery informs what you will read about here. Now that I'm in my 50s and have done a sizable piece of my own healing, I'm amazed at the ingenuity of my younger self. I tried many of the best cultural strategies that were available to me: I practiced staying ahead of it, disconnected from the worst parts of it, learned how to self-erase, grew the parts of me where I could find peace and competence, and connected with people and systems who could help me nearly perfect my earliest survival strategies. None of these early strategies helped me heal. They allowed me to survive long enough to start healing.

Carrying trauma necessitates survival strategies. The same cultures that wound us construct obstacles to healing. They dictate our options for survival and recovery. They instruct us on how we should best carry the wounds they give us. They shape which healing strategies "make sense" and which are "woo-woo." Many of us have survived by using culturally available survival and healing strategies. These include, but are not limited to, the following:

- Trying to Make Sense of the Trauma/Ruminating
- Forgiveness of Abusers
- Trying to Be Understood by Abusers
- Emotionally/Somatically Numbing Strategies
- Intellectualizing
- Dissociating from the Reality of It
- Trying to Be Loved Whole
- Trying to Love Someone Else Whole/Caretaking
- Giving It to God
- Repetition Compulsion
- Controlling Self, Others, or Things
- Mindfulness/Emotion Regulation Strategies
- Staying Ahead of It/Distracting Ourselves from It
- Making Ourselves Relevant to Others
- Telling the Story
- Addictions

None of these strategies reliably and predictably resolve the experiences that accumulate into complex trauma. Many of them result in additional traumatization. I tried many of them, and they represented much of the best cultural wisdom accessible when I was younger.

In 1991, when I could have most used a trauma-focused guide, I am certain that there was not a single therapist within 200 miles of me in rural Louisiana who had a single solid idea about how humans actually heal. Even in 2024, only a small percentage of therapists in the United States practice transformational trauma therapies with any regularity. Culturally, we are becoming more trauma-aware, but too few of us have any workable understanding of how healing actually happens. EMDR therapists sit a few feet from people who regularly and permanently resolve memories. We see clients astonish themselves every day. We once had a front-row seat to suffering; now we have a front-row seat to deep and astonishing healing. Even EMDR therapists struggle to explain clearly what we witness when we see clients recover from horror. Often, it simply feels like magic. One of the core arguments of this book is that magic is the least helpful, compelling, or sustaining metaphor. Once we see healing clearer, we can describe it better. We can be more precise about how our nervous systems learn. We can discover new and more efficient ways to heal.

Chapter 2
What if We've Been Overthinking It

How Humans Actually Heal

Neurobiology is largely the land of metaphor. "A knife cannot cut itself" is a metaphor, but an appropriate one here. EMDR therapy has been criticized in part because we cannot settle on a single workable mechanism of action. Yet, we have no idea what human consciousness is, neurobiologically speaking, or how it emerges. Any detailed understanding of human wounding and its resolution is unlikely to come in our lifetimes, but EMDR therapists regularly witness people heal from horrible experiences. From this vantage point, what can we know about how humans heal?

We are wounded experientially, and we heal experientially. It is difficult for me to imagine how healing might occur in other ways, having seen and experienced it so clearly through this lens. It is not controversial to argue that we are wounded experientially. Most therapists understand that much of the depression and most of the anxiety that we see in community mental health contexts are little more than the symptoms of deeply wounding experiences. EMDR therapy's Adaptive Information Processing (AIP) model places past experiences at the center of pathology and health.

It is more controversial to insist that we heal experientially.

A Remarkably Simple Concept

From Bruce Ecker (2024) comes a very simple concept. Humans heal when we activate a difficult experience and immediately have an experience that disconfirms the expectation in the bad memory. We must deeply experience the disconfirmation and not simply have a cognitive awareness of a mismatch. It is the *experience* of the disconfirmation that is transformational. However, EMDR therapists and Ecker are trying to shift very different types of information. Ecker is striving to construct experiences that will cause broad schema shifts all at once. EMDR therapists are simply trying to shift one memory. EMDR therapists evaluate schema shifts related only to the single memory we are processing. Ecker is trying to collapse an entire schema, such as "I don't matter," all in a single experience. Because we are trying to move different things, the precision of the disconfirmation is much more critical in Ecker's Coherence Therapy than in EMDR therapy and other memory-focused therapies. The key needed to unlock a bicycle is not the same one needed to access the Bank of America vaults in New York City. However, the central healing message remains: humans heal when they have experiences that disconfirm the expectation encoded in the bad memory.

This concept is not foreign. When we think about it, it is one of the ways that we have already assumed that humans might be able to heal. It is one of the assumptions that underlies many of our existing forms of coping, survival, regulating, and attempts to heal. As we will see, how we experience that disconfirmation matters.

EMDR Therapy

In nearly every transformational EMDR session, the client accesses a specific difficult memory and subsequently has a series of experiences that are different from (or disconfirming of) the expectation in the bad memory. Yes, the client experiences some sensations similar to those of the bad memory, but the client is guided to experience these sensations in the present moment (disconfirming) and in the presence of an attuned therapeutic relationship (also disconfirming). The client experiences himself interacting with the bad memory and noticing that it is easier and easier to tolerate it: "Look at me right here, right now, handling this." Noticing is inherently experiential. Experiential noticing is the enzyme that metabolizes information in EMDR therapy, and a lot of what is disconfirming is the experience that occurs when the difficult information makes contact with and is metabolized into the adaptive information already present in other parts of the client's system. Once the distress is fully digested, the client is invited to experience and notice holding together the positive cognition with the bad memory. The client then notices that she can put together the clear body scan, the memory, and the positive cognition all together and sit for a moment in that disconfirming experience. When EMDR therapy is transformational, it is experientially transformational, and those experiences always disconfirm the expectations in the bad memory.

Healing Relationally and Parts Work

We are wounded relationally. When we heal from relational wounds, disconfirming relational experiences are typically required. Parts work is a way for parts of us to have relational experiences with other parts of us that are different from the expectations in the bad memory. This may be why parts work itself can be healing. If our parts don't have experiences with each other in parts work that are different from the expectation in the bad memory, our parts work may not be productive (or worse, may reenact the dynamics of the traumatic experience). Parts of us introduce information to other parts of us. This information is metabolized through the disconfirmation of the interaction. Parts may be encouraged to engage with each other with curiosity and compassion rather than fear and blame.

The therapeutic relationship is also an opportunity for relational healing as the client experiences therapeutic interactions in ways that are different from the expectations in the bad experiences.

Somatic Interventions

Many somatic interventions encourage clients to experience body states and releases different from the expectations encoded in the bad experience. Again, humans heal when they have experiences different from the expectations in the bad memory.

EMDR 2.0

The working memory/disrupting working memory model is one of the hottest trends among EMDR therapists. Many EMDR therapists believe that the bilateral stimulation of EMDR therapy is an active ingredient in the efficacy of EMDR because of how it taxes working memory. However, watch closely the demos of EMDR 2.0. You will see that the distractions/disruptions of client focus cause the client to shift affective state rapidly. In short, the disruptions of focus cause clients to have experiences in the present that are so funny or so distracting that the client's experience in EMDR 2.0 is a disconfirmation of the expectation in the activated memory. The working mechanism in EMDR 2.0 may not be disruptions in working memory after all. The therapist-led disruptions may create conditions where the client has a different present experience with the bad memory, and that disconfirming experience causes the transformation of the bad memory.

Flash

Flash approaches are among the most explicit examples of activating a piece of memory content and guiding the client to have an experience that disconfirms the expectation in the bad memory. Clients are encouraged to micro-activate a single memory and then experience six back-to-back pleasant experiences that somatically disconfirm the expectation in the bad memory. The blinks in Flash split the 30-second exposure to the calm scene into six individual five-second micro-exposures to the calm scene, generating hundreds of disconfirming experiences in an average Flash session.

Summary

Clients with complex trauma rarely heal when they are presented with cognitive information alone. Useful information needs to be metabolized through experience. The interventions of therapy should be structured to promote and enhance disconfirming experiences.

When you have healed, how did you do it? What experiences were helpful in your healing journey?

Chapter 3
The Ethics of Not Treating Trauma

Almost any therapist who has ever worked in community mental health would quickly agree that most of the depression and most of the anxiety treated in these clinics is a byproduct of past wounding. When I ask a room filled with new EMDR trainees what percentage of their clients have experienced significant attachment wounding or horrible event trauma, the average percentage for each training is between 90% and 100%. However, the vast majority of mental health therapists are not trained in any form of trauma therapy, and fewer are trained in transformational trauma therapies.

It took several years after my EMDR foundational training before I met the first client who had ever engaged in any prior trauma work. I had a caseload filled with clients with significant trauma, and at least half of them had been in therapy for much of their lives. Very few of them had ever been diagnosed with PTSD by any prior therapist. They came to me with three to six other diagnoses. In reviewing the diagnostic assessments done by prior therapists, they reported multiple Criteria A PTSD events, and enough symptoms were reported to justify either a PTSD diagnosis or further exploration. Rarely was PTSD diagnosed, and nearly never was trauma an identified problem on the treatment plan. Why would a profession consistently assess something and then immediately disappear it as a subject of possible treatment?

I believe that it is an enormous individual and communal liability that most therapists do not know how to effectively treat one of the most common presenting issues to mental health clinics globally. This is not a defense against malpractice; it is the case for it.

The cultures around us are becoming more trauma-informed. As this happens, cultures expect accountability. They often want to know who knew what and when. They want to know who did something about it. All mental health clinics should be trauma centers. Trauma should not be a specialty. I have had therapists tell me with an absolutely congruous face, "I don't treat trauma." There is no avoiding it without substantial costs to our clients.

While we do need to train more trauma therapists, a more important task is to figure out how to keep more of the people we train. Our best research suggests that the vast majority of EMDR-trained therapists do not use it regularly. I suspect that most EMDR-trained therapists do not use EMDR therapy regularly with their clients because we don't train you to work with clients as complex as the ones you already treat. Clients with complex trauma are conceptualized as a special case, yet it is the only case that many of us will see. Treating clients with complex trauma is usually difficult for both clients and therapists. With the most complex clients, EMDR therapy is an 8.5 out of 10 difficult clinical task. This work is almost always really, really, hard. Don't let anyone convince you otherwise. Your clients need to heal, and there are no other professions that can do this work. Said differently, this work is squarely your job and your job only, so no one can save you from the need to learn to do it as well as you can. Working directly with trauma is easier than pretending that it is not in the room. There are substantial life consequences for clients who don't resolve trauma. There are ways to do this work more effectively.

Chapter 4
The Boat and the Whale Metaphor

Many trainees leave EMDR foundational therapy training with a core conceptual misunderstanding about what EMDR is. This misunderstanding causes some therapists to practice EMDR therapy in ways that may lead to therapist disillusionment with EMDR and in ways that could cause client harm. Trainers stress strict fidelity to standard protocol. This is sensible. It is important that trainees learn how to practice this therapy in standardized ways, in part so that they have a solid footing to make appropriate and clinically justified adjustments. Therapists tend to be creative people. It is very easy for a new trainee to get an initial understanding of EMDR and merge it with their understanding of Gestalt therapy, for example, and make a franken-therapy that is neither. However, what many trainees hear when trainers stress the importance of following standard protocol is: "If I don't do EMDR therapy in exactly this way, I'm doing it wrong and client harm is likely to occur." They hear this as though EMDR therapy is the recitation of specific words in a specific order. EMDR therapy is not a spell or incantation that loses its power if it is not performed perfectly. EMDR therapy is not a magic wand. In fact, the word "magic" does not appear in any versions of the Adaptive Information Processing model. When it works, EMDR therapy facilitates the linkage of stuck information into existing adaptive information that is already present somewhere in the client. EMDR therapy is an information processing therapy.

Phase One Is Also an Assessment of Adaptive Information

When I meet a client for the first time, I never know what difficulties they have encountered in life. From an EMDR therapy lens, I'm as interested in what has gone well in the client's life as I am in what has wounded him. Why? I have a general understanding of how difficult experiences might get better by using the Eight Phase Protocol of EMDR therapy. What I do not know is what the difficult information will connect to and metabolize into. Again, EMDR therapy does not simply desensitize a traumatic memory. It reprocesses the memory by connecting it to existing adaptive information. You cannot connect something to nothing in EMDR therapy, nor can you connect a lie to a lie.

You Can't Land a Whale Into a Canoe

The core of the AIP model is that we are connecting information to other information when engaging in EMDR therapy. Enough of the needed adaptive information must be present somewhere in the client's system for memory resolution to occur. Metaphorically, you cannot land a memory the size of a whale into adaptive information the size of a canoe. There is nothing magical in the Eight Phase Protocol that will automatically generate the needed adaptive information if it is not already there. Said differently, you do not get a bigger boat just because you are connected to a huge fish.

Clients with attachment wounding, developmental trauma, or complex trauma often have been too saturated with the tasks of survival to have had the opportunity to develop large amounts of adaptive information. One way of conceptualizing complex trauma is through the lens of the deficits of adaptive information. Clients with complex trauma typically have small boats of adaptive information and have oceans filled with massive monsters. They also have small windows of tolerance. Deficits in adaptive information and a narrow window of tolerance will and should directly impact how we conduct EMDR therapy with these clients.

Clients who have had great lives and securely attached childhoods typically have enormous amounts of adaptive information. It is easy to believe the lessons in your earliest nostalgia when those lessons are "your needs matter," "what you want is important," "you belong here," and "what you are feeling is real and matters to me." Clients who have had great lives have adaptive information the size of a cruise ship. People who have had good lives typically have a large window of tolerance. With their enormous foundation of adaptive information and their large window of tolerance, they can hook and land every fish in their oceans all at once.

This is the privilege of the non-pervasively traumatized. They do not have monsters in their oceans.

Implications

All aspects of EMDR therapy are affected by the presence or absence of adaptive information, as well as the traumatic load that the client is carrying. When clients have adaptive information the size of cruise ships, we typically do EMDR therapy with high fidelity to our initial training. We identify the memories relevant to the current dysfunction and often process them in the order of the largest first. It is important that therapists do not micromanage the work of recovery for the healthiest clients we see. A lot of their healing consists of seeing the relationship between their categories of wounding. We do not want to construct obstacles for that. In short, we need to trust the healthiest clients to let things go where they go.

For clients with extreme trauma and very little accessible adaptive information, letting things go where they go may encourage them to go straight off a cliff and may result in client harm, even if you do EMDR therapy exactly as you were trained. Complex trauma often requires sensible modifications to standard protocol. This is not particularly controversial. Sensible modifications may be necessary for complex trauma clients to successfully start somewhere. The following are just some of the sensible adjustments for working with complex trauma that you will learn about in this book:

- How to do Phase One with a client with 28,931 horrible memories.
- What a comprehensive-enough Phase Two look like.
- What does prepared to start mean?
- Selecting landable target memories.
- How we interact with the memory in Phase Four matters.
- Where processing tends to break and how to fix it.
- The things that resolving memories will not give you.

Chapter 5
EMDR Is Not a Magic Wand

Prior to training in EMDR therapy, most therapists had little prior experience with transformational trauma therapies. Throughout this book, transformational trauma therapies are defined as any approach that has a likelihood of fully and permanently resolving a target memory in a session or two. Many therapists (although certainly not all) observed their practicum partners during EMDR training resolve memories in ways that were astonishing. They may have experienced this themselves in the client role. Many first-time EMDR clients describe the process as magical. Getting past something is certainly novel and is itself a remarkable and disconfirming experience for many people.

The Bilateral Stimulation Is Not a Magic Wand

Much of the historical focus on EMDR therapy has been on its most culturally "weird" component: the bilateral stimulation, which is often performed in the form of left-right eye movements. Practitioners discovered soon after EMDR's development that many other forms of left-right stimulation are also effective in EMDR therapy, although the bilateral stimulation component remains its most distinctive and culturally weird feature. Some therapists assume that the active ingredient in EMDR therapy is the left-right stimulation, as though bilateral stimulation alone is inherently healing. Clearly, it is not. Otherwise, drummers would be the healthiest people on the planet. The history of rock-and-roll provides a compelling refutation of that assertion.

EMDR therapy consists of three core components: activation of a part of specific memory content, deep present-based noticing of the content that emerges, and while the client is engaging in left-right stimulation. I think of these components as three wheels of the tricycle of EMDR therapy, with the big front wheel being present-based noticing, since that is the component with the most contact and expenditure of effort. We need all three wheels for the tricycle to roll effectively. It makes no more sense to describe the rear right wheel as more central to the workings of EMDR than any of the other essential elements. Again, it takes all three. We will return later to the tricycle metaphor of EMDR therapy as a lens for exploring the problems that may emerge in this psychotherapy by exploring its discrete components.

If EMDR Is a Magic Wand, But It Does Not Work in My Hand

Many new EMDR therapists with a magic wand perspective encounter sessions where the opposite of magic occurs. The client may encounter real and intolerable distress that resists management and in ways that may scare both the client and the therapist. As is common in many bad relationships with a person or an idea, when an interaction goes sour we may conclude that we did something wrong or maybe that the magic wand does not work only when held in our hands. We did not get into this work to cause harm, yet the distressing fire that the client experienced in and after the session clearly traces back to the match in the therapist's hand. The advantage of removing magic from the equation in EMDR therapy is that we are not responsible for either its presence or its absence. Centering what is amazing and what is challenging in EMDR therapy inside the client's own complex and unique nervous system allows us to learn the lesson it needs to communicate. This learning allows us to make sensible adjustments to help our clients do this work in more productive and tolerable ways.

Chapter 6
No Part of This is Easy

With some trainees, something happens in six days of EMDR training that encourages them to lose track of the lessons of tens of thousands of hours that they have experienced with clients with complex trauma. EMDR trainees who have worked as therapists in community health contexts for ten years prior to getting trained in EMDR therapy have probably spent 16,000 hours in sessions with clients with severe and complex wounding. That's more direct exposure to anything else in their lives, other than perhaps media or their children. No one on the planet understands the complexity, nuances, and difficulties of working with complex clients more than community mental health workers. Nearly every intervention they have ever conducted has been slow, difficult, challenging, and required substantial modifications to be effective.

Working with clients with severe wounding is almost always hard. You already knew this. It's a lesson that we learned from the first week of our internship placements in graduate school and has been reinforced every session since. Working with clients with complex trauma in EMDR therapy is almost always hard. Pretending that we can ignore everything that we already know about working with complex trauma will make it much more difficult.

EMDR therapy may be intentionally or unintentionally marketed as an easy intervention. We may have been sold a version of ease. We were instructed in how to easily floatback a lifetime of wounding to just a few core memories and encouraged to start there after about a session of resourcing. Really, we should have known better. How we do EMDR therapy needs to be heavily informed by everything we already know about complex trauma, not the reverse.

Chapter 7
Therapist Anxiety

It is normal to have anxiety when we learn something new. If that new thing has real risks for real people that we care about, the anxiety may be even more acute. Often, we have to learn the lessons over and over again that 1) we can learn new things, 2) we become better and better at the things we do often, and 3) the stress related to new things gets better the more time passes in our engagement with it. In short, your comfort with EMDR therapy with complex clients will get better the same way every other thing you have ever accomplished gets better. It just takes time and practice. All the time and practice in the world will not make this work effortless or easy with clients with complex trauma. This is just a little reminder that I hope finds you on a day when you lose track of what makes you remarkable at what you do: you can be good at something and that thing can also be really difficult.

I still remember the days after my Part II EMDR training when several of my clients fell into the quicksand of attachment wounds, and I did not know how to help them. Every resource I tried wasn't helpful. I remember driving home sad and frustrated. Some of the client's existential loneliness that filled the room was still sitting in my chest and stomach. I have a clear memory of driving past a field of cows and yelling out loud: "F* trauma!" "F* EMDR!" "I should have been an accountant!" "I should just drive a UPS truck!" There will be days like this. Now, I can look back with gratitude for those difficult sessions and the important information they communicated. These experiences have instructed, shaped, and cultivated the words in this book. These difficult days will make you a better EMDR therapist, assuming you find strategies to navigate them.

Chapter 8
What Makes Complex Trauma So Complex for EMDR Therapy?

Volumes have been written about the complexity of trauma when it impacts multiple developmental eras and intersects core developmental needs. This section is about the relevance of complex trauma for the tasks specifically required to do EMDR therapy well. Returning to the Tricycle metaphor to describe the central features of EMDR therapy, activation is the rear left wheel, noticing the activation is the front center wheel, and left-right stimulation is the back right wheel.

Activation is a core task in most transformational trauma therapies. EMDR therapy is complicated by the large number of memories that will need to be processed. Figuring out where to start with clients with complex trauma can be a more complicated clinical task. It is wise to start work at the intersection of what is productive and what is tolerable. Also, clients with complex trauma will need to be able to activate a part of a difficult memory. Some clients are too shut down to activate. Others may have blocking beliefs related to emotional expression, which may directly impact their capacity to activate. We need distress to come, but it needs to come in discrete chunks small enough for the client's current window of tolerance and should be tolerable enough for the client to notice in the present. The memory content should not come into awareness faster or with more intensity than clients can notice. Also, the memory content needs to be at least somewhat limited to prevent a large number of adjacent memories from coming into awareness. Because EMDR therapy encourages distress to form and sit in the body, the familiarity of the body-based sensations can cause adjacent memories to want to come into awareness resulting in many memories coming into awareness at a rate faster than the client can metabolize any of them.

In general, clients will most commonly struggle in EMDR therapy when memory content comes into awareness at a rate or intensity faster than they can notice and digest. Content and distress do not want to come in modest pieces with clients with complex trauma. Their nervous system wants to swing out into the deep end of it.

In many ways, noticing is the bright yellow line in the center of the EMDR road. Noticing requires the capacity to slow down and be present.

Slowing down is particularly complicated for people whose core survival strategy has been to stay ahead of it. Present awareness is very difficult for many clients with complex trauma because the present is where everything bad happens. Asking clients with complex trauma to slow down, be present, and notice in an activated state is to ask them to engage in a trifecta of triggering.

We are always connecting difficult information to other, more adaptive information that is present somewhere in the client's system in EMDR therapy. Clients with complex trauma typically have large amounts of difficult experiences, but very little adaptive information for the difficult experiences to connect with and metabolize into. We cannot connect a lie to a lie and we cannot metabolize difficult information into nothing. The information necessary for healing needs to be already present in the client. If it isn't, we need to help clients develop it. Our interventions should help the client have experiences in session and between sessions that help build or support adaptive information.

Chapter 9
All the Hats You Wear

The clients who most motivated you to start your EMDR journey may be the clients whom you do the least reprocessing with, especially early on. This is an unfortunate but common reality. Your clients with the most extensive trauma are likely to have the most needs of you. You already wear a lot of hats when working with clients with complex trauma, and now add EMDR therapy to the multitude of hats you wear.

Do you know what happens in an average week between sessions with your healthiest clients? Not much. That is part of the fortune of the non-pervasively traumatized. Trauma doesn't endlessly happen to them. What happens in an average week between sessions with your clients with complex trauma? Typically, an enormous amount. They may have housing crises, relational crises, deaths, family or community violence, and physical health issues, some of which may need attending to outside of EMDR therapy. When someone doesn't have anyone in their life to listen to them with compassion, attunement is a trauma-focused intervention in the service of survival. However, our clients also need to heal. We feel the desperate need for the client to heal, sometimes with more urgency than the client is aware of that need in themselves.

Your clients with the highest traumatic load are often those with the least accessible resources and may be the most difficult to resource. Resourcing can take months. It is difficult to prepare a client for the EMDR journey when present life stressors have saturated them. Doing EMDR therapy well requires the capacity for the client to feel worse for a little while. If the client is already at the bottom of the pool, we cannot ask them to dive deeper today. Our interventions in such sessions have to be focused on helping them up and helping to support enough stability so that they can develop a capacity to slow down, be present, and notice. EMDR therapy requires a window of tolerance. We will explore ways to widen the window of tolerance and other ways to help distress ripple inside of it, rather than distress coming like a tsunami and overtopping it.

Chapter 10
How We Train You

We do not train you to work with clients with complex trauma. We train you to work with someone who is relatively healthy, has adaptive information, knows how to notice, is embodied enough to notice, and has the emotional capacity to activate and tolerate deeply noticing present distress. We train you to work with the type of clients who rarely show up at the agencies where you work. The clients who do show at community mental health agencies typically have pervasively traumatized nervous systems, decades of severe event trauma, childhoods filled with unmet developmental needs (thus significant confusion about those needs), few adaptive coping strategies, and profound deficits in insight and adaptive information. In short, EMDR therapy was not developed using clients with the severity and acuity of trauma that many of you treat on a daily basis.

Shapiro conceptualizes EMDR therapy as a brief approach to psychotherapy. Her initial research reinforced her central assertion that EMDR therapy is effective and efficient. However, there are no brief approaches to psychotherapy adequate to treat decades of daily, severe, and pervasive wounding. EMDR therapy is an effective way to treat clients with complex trauma, but no therapy will ever be both brief and comprehensive with complex trauma. The imprints of severe trauma are deep and redundantly placed. Hundreds of thousands of years of survival instinct are organized around the imperative to attend to the lessons taught by awfulness. These lessons aren't meant to be unlearned with ease.

We have remarkably few ways to heal. EMDR therapy is one of those few ways. I cannot accept that EMDR therapy is a way that humans can heal, yet deny this treatment to the people who most need to heal simply because they do not meet the metrics of a healthy nervous system. If EMDR therapy was not developed using this population, our use necessitates finding and utilizing reasonable adjustments that allow us to retain the central qualities of what makes EMDR therapy effective. Shapiro recommends many modifications for clients with complex trauma. In fact, Francine Shapiro is not nearly the Shapiro purist that many trainers and consultants suggest. A close reading of Shapiro's (2018) book finds her pointing to many of the territories that are identified, explored, and expanded upon here.

My goal is to help you leverage what you already know about complex trauma and to help you shape your interventions to match the unique qualities and realities of your client's nervous system. This is the essence of solid, effective, and efficient clinical practice. To do otherwise is to attempt to shove our clients with complex trauma through a machine built for someone with a completely different shape.

Phase One

"The only line that is true is the line you're from."

--Blind Pilot, "One Red Thread"

Chapter 11
Doing a Sensible Phase One

Shapiro (2018) describes several approaches to Phase One of EMDR therapy. They are all appropriate and reasonable for people who have had generally good lives but have experienced some trauma. Quickly identifying those experiences and developing a plan to resolve them (probably starting with the worst first) is the most efficient way to work with generally healthy people.

These Shapiro approaches to Phase One are not ideal for many people whose whole life has been awful. With clients with severe and complex trauma, I am not focused on the most efficient way possible to resolve a limited number of memories. I anticipate that these clients will need to be on my caseload for a few years and we may need to resolve 80 memories or more. Complex trauma is that complex. In fact, a few years of weekly therapy may not be enough for some. My focus and urgency are adequately preparing the client to start somewhere. The risk is that we never start at all.

Multiple things that appear to conflict can be true at the same time. How we approach clients who are healthy is different from how we approach clients who have pervasively traumatized nervous systems. This is true of every approach to psychotherapy. EMDR therapy is no exception. On second thought, because EMDR therapy has a way of quickly and directly floating back issues to the experiences that are central and potentially volatile, we should perhaps be more careful about what we activate in the sessions before the client has the capacity to manage any of that activation.

I invite you to go on a mental journey with me. For a moment, please rewind to the day before you started the first day of your Part One EMDR training. Subtract everything from your awareness that you now know about EMDR therapy. Many of you had been working with complex trauma for months, years, or decades prior to taking your EMDR training. Think about everything you know about complex trauma from sitting with many clients across hundreds, thousands, or tens of thousands of sessions. Would it make sense to ask them to touch three, nine, or 27 of the worst and most unspeakable experiences that could possibly happen to a single person on this planet? Is getting a detailed and comprehensive trauma history the first time you meet a person with extreme trauma a trauma-informed intervention based on what we know about how trauma is stored and how it might be activated even from gentle inquiry? Is asking a client who has been complexly wounded to tell you ten of the worst things that have happened to her the moment you first meet her something that a decent person does to another person? Before you participated in an EMDR training, would exploring trauma in this way have been a reasonable, appropriate, and trauma-informed approach with a client who is probably coming to this first therapy session as an act of survival? If it isn't, what is it about EMDR therapy that makes this seem like a good idea? Why do you need to know these details on first contact? Is it because you think EMDR is a magic wand? Is it because you think EMDR therapists somehow have ways of exploring trauma histories that don't risk over-activation? Or are you trying to do a detailed Phase One with clients with extreme trauma because that's how we trained you to do it (even though parts of you already know that's probably a really bad idea)? Please, don't do things with clients with complex trauma in EMDR therapy that your years of clinical expertise suggest is a horrible idea. Everything you know about complex trauma should heavily inform how you do EMDR therapy. It should make you a better EMDR therapist. You shouldn't have to forget anything you know about complex trauma in order to do EMDR therapy well or "correctly."

To be fair, Shapiro repeatedly reassures us that we can do a comprehensive Phase Two before we do a comprehensive Phase One, if that is appropriate. However, that does not match the agency and billing mandates that shape how many of us are forced to practice. We typically need to develop a treatment plan within the first session or two, and that treatment plan has to capture the presenting issues, symptoms, history, severity, diagnosis, approach, and concrete goals and objectives for therapy. In short, we do not have the time, resources, or stability needed to do Phase One in many of the ways that Shapiro envisions immediately, yet we still need to get information that will allow us to conceptualize the client's case and develop an initial approach to treatment.

If we can agree that we should have additional options for working with severely traumatized clients on our first few contacts, perhaps we should explore what those options might look like.

Some Options for Phase One for Agency Contexts

If you work at a community mental health agency, you will probably need to do an intake and symptom-based treatment plan in the way the agency requires. You will usually need to get metrics to support the diagnosis and you can use many of these metrics (anxiety, depression, or trauma assessments) to build a trauma-focused treatment plan. If you intend to do EMDR therapy with your clients who do not currently meet the criteria for PTSD, it is important to make sure that your initial treatment plan conceptualizes the current symptoms as trauma symptoms through the AIP model lens, meaning that these symptoms are the result of difficult past experiences or learning. A symptom-based treatment plan that anticipates the need for a comprehensive Phase Two; anticipates further exploration of specific target memories related to the presenting issues; includes a plan to target (currently unnamed) central memories implicated in the development and maintenance of the current issue; and the plan to do future templates to leverage work conducted with past memories is a workable way to get started. The treatment plan should also include many of the other non-EMDR interventions that you may anticipate utilizing. Again, clients with complex trauma often have complex needs and you will wear the most hats with these clients. The treatment plan can always be revised as additional information becomes available.

The "Buckets" of Wounding often Emerge Organically

When conducting a treatment plan in this way, it is highly likely that you will start to get a sense of the broad categories or "buckets" of wounding that the client has encountered at different developmental eras organically. For instance, you may become aware of the presence of developmental trauma, difficulty in early dating relationships, or an abusive first marriage. From there you can start to get a glimpse of other ways that the past may be affecting the present quality of life. Clients can often connect current symptoms to past developmental eras in ways that are helpful but do not necessarily include specific and potentially activating memory content.

Phase One Should Also Assess for Adaptive Information

It is important to remember that we need to assess for the presence of adaptive information, since adaptive information is the "boat" that the difficult memories will need to be landed into. A simple way to think about adaptive information is: What has the client learned about himself and the world outside of the lessons of the trauma? Sometimes having our own children can teach us about the things that humans are born needing, when our own childhoods did not provide that information. On occasion, clients with complex trauma may find fortune in love and have a long-term relationship with someone who is kind, patient, and loving. We can explore ways that these experiences have provided corrective information for trauma learning. The most usable adaptive information is best learned experientially. From what you have learned about this client's life, when would they have had the opportunity to develop the needed adaptive information? Also, adaptive information isn't one thing. Some clients may have large amounts of adaptive information for one category of belief about the self, but severely lack it for others.

Using Resources to Assess for Potential Somatic Deficits

It is possible to use some initial resourcing exercises as a way to get important information about the state of the client's nervous system, and this information can be incorporated into the treatment plan. In addition to assessing existing resources that the client may have, it can be helpful to assess for embodiment as soon as possible. I typically do a quick body scan (see Chapter 21: Dip Your Toe In Body Scan) to assess for somatic dissociation. If the client appears to have poor awareness of how stressors are embodied, body awareness exercises may be incorporated as interventions in the treatment plan in preparation for the EMDR processing phases.

Helpful Assessment Instruments

It can be helpful to obtain metrics of trauma symptoms and do so in ways that are not overly triggering. The PCL-5 is a helpful public-domain instrument. While not a diagnostic instrument, the Dissociative Experiences Scale (DES-II) can be a helpful survey of dissociation symptoms. Trauma approached from an AIP model lens conceptualizes most depression and nearly all anxiety as symptoms of past wounding. Thus, standard anxiety and depression inventories can be helpful trauma metrics to include in treatment planning.

Helpful Intake and Treatment Planning Questions

One of the most important questions in my intake sessions is to assesses for attachment wounding. Attachment wounds are often the whales of memory. Some of the most difficult sessions I have witnessed in EMDR therapy involve attachment wound targets. Events have a beginning, middle, and end. Attachment wounds are about everything. They are about belonging, connection, family, safety, identity, importance, and value. Attachment wounds have compounding costs developmentally because: not getting our needs met was wounding, we were often blamed for having those needs (which is also wounding), we had to develop coping strategies to cope with those unmet needs (which typically have long-term costs), and we may be missing a lot of the implicit learning (adaptive information) that getting our needs met would have provided. Not having the experience of this adaptive learning tends to be both informationally and developmentally stunting.

The question I ask is simply, **"When you were young, who was really and consistently there for you?"** The consistency part is important. The client may have had a fantastic grandmother, but she may have lived hundreds of miles away. Consistency is also important for people who were physically present. Inconsistent attachment is the foundation of some of the most difficult and deeply complex presentations that we encounter clinically.

When a client answers the above question with "no one," they will do so in less than a second. This math was conducted by the client's nervous system a long time ago. It's one of the truest things that they know. I know then that we will attempt to develop an attachment figure resource or do other forms of targeted parts work to create and model the possibility of self-nurture and more effective self-communication. When clients grow up in a context of insecure attachment, assume that significant developmental deficits exist that will likely impact the client's current fund of adaptive information.

It can be helpful to do a general survey of childhood for the client's gut-level impression of difficulty without asking about individual experiences or memories. I will do this by asking the following questions:

Without thinking about any specific memories, but just checking your gut-level impression, how difficult was life for you before five years old on a ten-point scale?

Between five and ten years old?
Between ten and 15 years old?
Between 15 and 20?
Between 20 and 30? Etc.

It is possible to get a very general overview of the extent of wounding in the lifespan from this simple, and generally non-triggering, way of inquiring. When I ask these questions, it is easy for me to form a mental line chart in my mind (similar to the figures below) of the client's impression of life difficulty by age range. Severe stressors in very early to middle childhood generally result in significant dysfunction in later life. I anticipate a much longer and more complicated course of treatment for the client on the left than the right. I anticipate that the client on the left may have substantial deficits in adaptive information because of the ways that the difficulty of early experiences may have been developmentally disrupting.

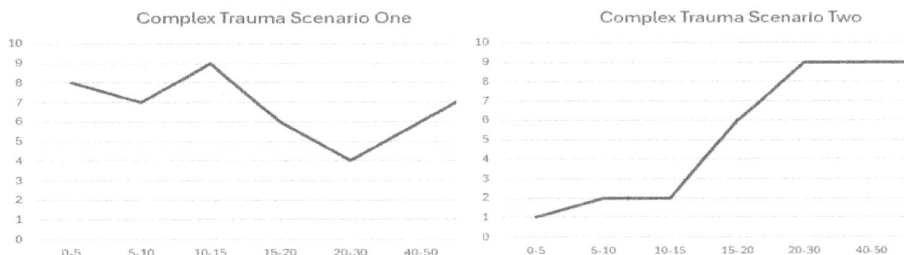

Chapter 12
How Exactly Should We Do Phase One?

You may have noticed that the Phase Two part of this book starts on the next page. Some of you may be wondering when I'm going to tell you exactly how to do Phase One with all your clients with complex trauma. I hear you murmuring, "Tom, you have told me what not to do. You have told me not to make a big list of all the horrible stuff all at once. You have a few areas of inquiry that you suggest. You have said that I should be trauma-informed and sensitive in my approaches… but I don't know what to *do* for Phase One."

I'm only going to humbly suggest that you do know what to do. You know how to begin therapy with clients with severe trauma. They sit in front of you, and they try to find the words that explain why they are there. They don't tell you everything you need to know to fully conceptualize the case the first time you meet them, because how could they? You do not have everything that you need to fully conceptualize their case in the first session or two, because how could you? You will start Phase One by starting. You will listen closely and warmly and you will figure out how to start therapy at the intersection of what might be productive for them and what might also be tolerable for them. Maybe you don't need to start in a way any more complicated than that. I can promise, the next session and the next will bring more essential information. That information also becomes part of your stretched-out Phase One of understanding more deeply and richly who this client is, what they have survived, what they have learned, and where their unburdening might most productively and tolerably begin. The goal of Phase One with clients with complex trauma is not to fully and conceptually organize their whole recovery at first contact. It is to build an adequate enough understanding to safely start somewhere. Again, one of the big risks is that we become so overwhelmed with everything that we don't ever start somewhere.

Phase Two

"This moment would define my memory of that night, and of the many nights like it, for a decade. In it I saw myself as unbreakable, as tender as stone. At first I merely believed this, until one day it became the truth. Then I was able to tell myself, without lying, that it didn't affect me, that he didn't affect me, because nothing affected me. I didn't understand how morbidly right I was. How I had hollowed myself out. For all my obsessing over the consequences of that night, I had misunderstood the vital truth: that its not affecting me, that was its effect."

–Tara Westover, *Educated*

Chapter 13
Phase Two Isn't Just Mindfulness Resources

Relatively healthy clients are resourced well by life. It is easy to believe the truths our bodies know about our earliest moments of connection with healthy attachment figures. If appropriate roles were modeled for us, we are less likely to be confused about what is uniquely ours and what legitimately belongs to others. It is easier for us to learn how to regulate if the people present in our earliest memories lived regulated lives and were able to successfully get between us and the harshest surfaces of the world. There is an enormous privilege in having a healthy nervous system. Much of what is needed in order to heal easily in EMDR therapy is already present and usable.

The information deficits that are created by attachment wounding, developmental disruptions, early childhood trauma, role confusion, and significant family dysfunction are substantial. Not only were the wrong things modeled, but their presence may have prevented us from having enough experiential learning with the good things. Often, central to complex trauma is the presence of things that should not have happened and the absence of things that should have happened. These conditions create voids in the very information networks that will be needed to resolve these experiences in EMDR therapy. The difficult experiences will resolve in EMDR therapy only if the system has enough of the needed adaptive information. Fortunately, even if childhood was horrible, it is possible to subsequently develop much of the needed adaptive information. Developing this information is generally more difficult and complicated the more unprecedented the adaptive information is to the client's system.

While Shapiro conceptualizes some of the tasks described in this chapter as Phase One work, this book conceptualizes all of the tasks of developing the needed adaptive information squarely as Phase Two work since they are all conducted to enhance preparation for more effective processing in EMDR therapy.

Understanding Trauma

Many clients with complex trauma present with a poor understanding of the ways that trauma impacts the lifespan. They often come filled with the projections of family members or with the diagnostic labels assigned by mental health professionals, but usually have a limited understanding of how their "pathologies" are largely symptoms of what they have endured or what they have missed.

Clients with complex trauma will need to come to a workable understanding of trauma and its impacts. EMDR therapy is easiest to explain when built upon a solid understanding of trauma. It is an answer to the problem of trauma. Clients who don't conceptualize their problems as trauma symptoms may struggle to endorse the extended journey of recovery using EMDR therapy.

Before starting EMDR therapy, part of the adaptive information that is often needed is some shift away from the "I am the problem" to "what has happened to me is the problem" orientation for the client. We do not promote this shift as an attempt to deny any blame or accountability where these are appropriate, but to normalize and contextualize wounding and its aftermath truthfully and adaptively.

There are many ways to educate clients about trauma. If clients enjoy reading, sometimes non-clinical books and resources are appropriate. However, this work is best started in the therapy office and when it is done well, it can help enhance and solidify the therapeutic relationship.

Educate Clients About EMDR Therapy

EMDR therapy requires that clients go on this journey in a very specific and non-intuitive way. As we have explored elsewhere, EMDR therapy is a trifecta of cultural taboo: we purposefully activate traumatic information, encourage the client to notice in the present what comes up following that activation, and to do all this while the nervous system receives bilateral stimulation. Clients need to learn how to not activate memory content at a rate faster or more intense than they can digest. Clients need the capacity to be present, to notice deeply in the present, and they need to have a window of tolerance that is appropriate for the distress that comes into awareness and sits in the body.

There are many ways to educate clients about EMDR therapy. Again, this is best done after a solid orientation to trauma is provided. Some language that I often use is described in the following paragraph:

There is something about activating a piece of a difficult memory, noticing deeply what comes as a result of that activation, and doing so while you are receiving a left-right stimulation that helps shift a stuck memory in a way that makes it easier to carry. When we do EMDR therapy, we typically work on one memory at a time and we often work only one piece of it at a time. As soon as the preparation work is complete, we can start. I usually like to start somewhere small, so that we can practice it before working on things that are large.

Other explanations I have provided include this excerpt:

EMDR therapy allows your nervous system to digest what you were too overwhelmed, shut down, or didn't have the information needed to digest at the time the experience happened. When everything is in place to start this work, I'll help you select a memory that feels tolerable for you to start. You will spend most of the session simply noticing what comes up while you are engaging in a left-right stimulation that should help you stay in the present and promote the movement of each piece of stuck information.

I also walk the client through all eight phases (including the Phase Three-Seven script) of the EMDR protocol so that they can clearly see what EMDR therapy is and what will be required of them.

I inform clients clearly that we need the following things to be in place to do EMDR therapy well:

- A window of tolerance wide enough to allow you to notice in a tolerable way each aspect of the memory. We will provide resources to help you widen your window of tolerance.
- All noticing that is productive in EMDR therapy must happen in the present moment. We will work to support present-moment awareness as opposed to detailed awareness of what was happening at the time of the wounding experience.
- You will need to be embodied enough to notice. Many people with wounding learn to survive by somatically dissociating. We will work to help develop more body awareness if that is needed.
- Noticing is a very active verb in EMDR therapy. Noticing is more than simply being aware of something. Noticing in EMDR therapy requires slowing down and being present with the distress or other

content that is coming into awareness or that has gathered in the body or system. If needed, we will do exercises that help strengthen your capacity to notice deeply.
- Enough adaptive information needs to be present for the difficult information to connect to and metabolize into. Enough of the adaptive information needed to resolve a memory needs to be present somewhere in the system. When EMDR therapy is successful, we are always connecting stuck information to existing adaptive information. We cannot connect a lie to a lie.

I will expand on each of the above points more in the sections below, and many are covered in their own chapters. Again, it is important to explain what EMDR therapy is so that clients can clearly understand why you are asking them to engage in periods of extended resourcing. If you are able to clearly specify the requirements for doing EMDR therapy well and safely, then you and the client can continue to evaluate if deficits are present. It is not enough to simply declare that a client isn't prepared to do EMDR therapy processing phases, as a carnival worker might measure the head of a child against a fixed height line and continually declare him too short to ride a carnival ride. Resourcing must proactively address the deficits that are present; otherwise, you risk endlessly returning the client to Phase Two, where all hope of actually doing EMDR therapy will go to die.

A Wide Enough Window of Tolerance

We need distress to come in EMDR therapy, but it needs to come into awareness at a digestible amount and intensity. Many clients with complex trauma present at an average session with a baseline 8/10 level of stress/distress prior to starting any target memory, and this baseline level of distress may be a substantial improvement over their initial baseline level of stress/distress at intake. Clients who simply do not have the capacity to feel worse on any given day are not good candidates for EMDR therapy on that day unless we are able to help them substantially reset prior to reprocessing (which is unlikely).

Part of our job early in treatment is to help the client expand their window of tolerance. There are many ways to do this, including the following options:

- Help the client better manage acute stressors that may be causing or feeding current instability.
- Use resources to help the client have repeated experiences where their nervous system can experience a slight and brief decrease in body-based stress. The experiences show the client's system that they can still be safe at a slightly lower level of arousal and this expanding range of safety may start to lower baseline anxiety.
- Connect to existing resources that may be currently underutilized.

We will discuss strategies in the book to make the most of a narrow window of tolerance in processing, but a primary goal of Phase Two is to widen it as much as possible prior to engaging in processing.

The Present Moment Needs to be Safe Enough

All noticing that is productive in EMDR therapy needs to happen in the present moment and in the right-now body. For many people with complex trauma, the present is not safe. Obviously, many people with complex trauma continue to live or work in unsafe environments. Even when nothing bad is happening or at significant risk of happening, the present moment is not experienced as safe. Many clients dissociate into the worst parts of the past and the worst worries of the future to escape the present moment. I had a client once say that he would rather me set him on fire than ask him to be present in the present and notice something.

A core survival strategy for many people is to stay ahead of it... whatever their *it* in trauma is. When we do exercises with clients that invite present awareness, often their anxiety skyrockets. They often blame the resource, but the problem is at least partly a near-phobic response to slowing down, being present, and noticing. For clients with trauma, everything bad happened in the present. The present is no more neutral territory than the body is. And when they are present, there is often a strong feeling that everything that they have tried to stay ahead of might start to catch up to them.

In order for EMDR therapy to be effective, we need to help make the present moment safe enough to embody and notice during reprocessing. We attempt this by constructing experiences where the client is able to briefly bring awareness to the present and notice in very concrete ways. The "Dip Your Toe In" resources in this section are an excellent place to start doing this work. Exploring times when the client is able to safely feel more present and use those as anchors is helpful (you can slow-tap the memory of these experiences in as resources if they feel adaptive). We can also encourage the client to engage in those organic resources even more frequently during this phase.

Again, if we are going to ask a client to slow down, be present, and notice distress for 40 or more minutes in a session, we need to make sure that the present is a tolerable-enough place for the client. If it is not, then we need to try to help make present awareness safer if we intend to do EMDR therapy processing phases.

Clients Need to Be Embodied Enough to Notice

EMDR is a somatic psychotherapy. In the van der Kolk (2014) conceptualization, EMDR therapy is a bottom-up intervention. For EMDR therapy to be effective, you need to be in your bottom (body) enough to notice. However, you do not need to be a mindfulness guru.

Somatic dissociation is often a trauma survival strategy when information from the body wasn't helpful for providing safety. In the cultures where I work, many men are somatically dissociated. They were raised in cultures where the only emotions that were not shamed out of them were anger and sports joy. We will explore in other chapters how to promote body awareness. However, by the time we have arrived in Phase Two, you should have assessed for somatic awareness using body scans. You can also get clues to it from the client's reported response to mindful resources.

EMDR therapy is not a power think-think session with left-right stimulation. How are emotions experienced when a client is somatically dissociated? They are experienced as thoughts about feelings. When you ask, clients will often preface the response with, "I think I would feel…" With many clients who are disconnected from their bodies, you can help them become more embodied by having them do a "Dip Your Toe In" body scan, engage in a mindfulness exercise, then repeat the body scan. Encourage the client to repeat this several times a day. Tasking the parts of the brain responsible for monitoring the body in the present can be helpful in promoting more body awareness.

The Client Needs to Know How to Notice

Many clients with complex trauma will have no idea what you mean when you invite them to "notice" something internally. Approaching the body or experience from a place of curiosity is not generally something that has been asked of them before. Learning how to ignore body sensations when those sensations are distressing or did not contain information helpful for survival is an understandable adaptation to trauma.

Noticing is the bright yellow line in the center of the EMDR road. When clients lose track of that task, there is no telling where EMDR therapy will take them, but it probably will not be to a productive place. Returning to the Tricycle metaphor developed earlier, noticing is the front center wheel on the tricycle because it is the task that clients are engaged in the most and where the majority of their efforts are spent. The task of noticing is introduced in Phase Two so that we can do it more easily and effortlessly in Phases Four-Six.

To help clients develop awareness of body sensations, I may give the client the following guidance when noticing something pleasant:

> Scan your body and notice anything that is pleasant emerging from this resource. Observe its qualities. Does it have a shape, texture, temperature, impulse, or intensity? Just notice any qualities of it that are present, even for just a moment.

In preparation for the processing phases, explore what I mean by body-based noticing:

> Scan your body and find the place of most distress and notice the qualities of that sensation. Is it still or moving? Notice its size and notice its boundary or its shape. Does it have a temperature or a texture? Is it heavy or is it empty? Notice its inside. Notice its qualities like you are about to draw or sketch it. When it changes, just follow it with your awareness.

The Client Needs Enough Adaptive Information

When EMDR therapy is effective, we are connecting stuck information into other adaptive information. Information connects to information in EMDR therapy. The information that is required for your healing needs to already be inside you and accessible to the parts of you that need to access it.

While there are many exceptions, it is common that the needed adaptive information may be held in the most resourced, adult, and "neocortex" parts. These may also be the parts that will struggle to be online and accessible when clients are flooded, otherwise overactivated, or dissociated from the present moment. Strategies that help clients stay well within the window of tolerance also help parts of the brain communicate more easily with other parts, generally producing faster and more tolerable healing in EMDR therapy.

When it becomes clear that clients do not have enough adaptive information present in a reprocessing session to metabolize the information in the trauma, it makes sense to pivot to closure. We may have already tried interweaves to target the very deficits that are implicated in the present block. If the block is related to guilt, shame, blame, responsibility we may have used perspective-taking interweaves (for more information on this see Chapter 41: Where Clients Get Stuck and How to Intervene). If the block to the information moving is an attachment wound, we will pivot to an attachment figure resource as a part of closure.

The following list contains some of the places where clients get stuck in deficits of accessible adaptive information:

- It is not safe for me to feel / I can't show my emotions
- I am responsible for what happened when I was a child
- The bad things happened because I am bad
- I should have known the bad thing would happen
- I didn't stop it, so I am responsible for it
- Not being loved consistently means that I am unlovable
- I cannot trust that people are actually there for me
- I cannot trust myself to know what is good, true, or safe
- I do not deserve to heal
- I cannot tolerate noticing certain body sensations
- Parts of me hate and resent the kid parts of me

I am not aware of any comprehensive, easy, and reliable screening of adaptive information that would indicate adequate informational health to start EMDR therapy. Many deficits in adaptive information are revealed in how clients talk about themselves and the world. Also, adaptive information is not one thing. What is needed to resolve one category of memory might be different from what could be needed to resolve a different memory. Also, remember that a validity of cognition (VOC) of one roughly means, "no part of me believes that the positive cognition might be true." A VOC of one does not necessarily mean that we should abandon working on a memory in Phase Three (although you might consider it if you confirm with a few clarifying questions related to the extremity of that belief).

Phase Two is often the most difficult phase of EMDR therapy. It is where the battle is won or lost. Hundreds of thousands of clients have seen EMDR-trained therapists and never moved past Phase Two. Without strategies to assess deficits and make concrete and sensible adjustments to address them, Phase Two is often where any hope of doing EMDR therapy goes to die.

Chapter 14
The Utility of Parts Work

If you are new to EMDR therapy, it must seem that "parts work" has suddenly dropped into EMDR Therapy as its latest fad, and clinicians are divided into assorted "denominations" about how to best do it with all the judgments and camp dogma that can come with it. This chapter explores parts work as a concept that has always been essential to EMDR therapy and is essential to doing EMDR therapy well. I'm not exploring here how to "do" parts work, rather I'm explaining why we're always doing parts work in EMDR therapy.

One of the many things that EMDR's AIP model does is that it describes what a difficult memory is. A traumatic memory contains the raw sensory information perceived by the nervous system at the time of the experience. It also contains a snapshot of you at the time the trauma happened: the perspectives through which you viewed yourself and the world. Also encoded in the memory are your affective states at the time of the trauma. It is also possible at the time of the trauma that the schema component of the memory (the take-home messages of fat, ugly, stupid, lazy, not safe, or my fault, etc.) get initially encoded. And if the schema components aren't inserted at the time of the trauma, then they will be as this experience gets brought into working memory and then returned back into the parts of the brain that store trauma over and over in the years or decades since. If a memory encapsulates all aspects of an event as it was experienced by the nervous system at that time, then we need to understand that this experience happened at a particular developmental era and was experienced by the parts system that existed at the time of the trauma. Encoded in many memories are worldviews, affects, internal conflicts, survival strategies, and parts. The parts in that memory have since evolved into the client's right-now parts. We are often working with two systems of parts: the parts at the time of the trauma and your right-now parts. We are working with the information accessible at the time of the trauma and the information that is accessible to you right now. The degree to which the parts systems are similar to each other or different depends largely on the nature of the experiences that you have had since the trauma. We are wounded through experiences and we heal experientially. We gain new information experientially. In EMDR therapy, healing is the connection between these two information systems. Healing can be complicated by internal conflicts between the right-now parts system, the trauma-era parts, or any conflicts between the parts systems.

At the core of the Adaptive Information Processing model is the idea that difficult experiences must connect to right-now existing adaptive information if healing occurs. I often use the metaphor of a boat and a fish, with the boat being the adaptive information and the fish being the memory information you are trying to land. In EMDR therapy, you can't land a fish bigger than your boat. In the most general sense, healthy people typically have healthy systems. They have boats the size of cruise ships. A lot of their healing requires that we stay out of their way and let them see the connection between various periods of wounding. Healthy people have enormous amounts of adaptive information and typically have large windows of tolerance. They can typically land every fish that they hook onto. People with pervasively traumatized nervous systems may not have had much of an opportunity to develop information different from the time of the trauma, and this is where parts work can be complicated. What do you do when the parts of you at the time of the trauma when you were six years old are convinced that the trauma is your fault, and the most grown-up right-now parts also believe that the trauma at six years old was your fault? In EMDR therapy, you can connect old stuck information into right-now adaptive information (if you have enough of it), but you can't connect a lie into a lie. It doesn't work in EMDR therapy. Most of the problems in EMDR therapy and all blocking beliefs aren't problems because the kid parts in the memory believe them. Rather, they are blocks because your right-now grown-up parts still believe those old lessons about yourself.

Parts work provides opportunities for your parts to have experiences that are different from the expectation in the bad memory. For some people, these are some of their first experiments in self-compassion. They are some of the first experiences of parts of you extending compassion to other parts of you. In many forms of parts work, one part of you (typically a more resourced part) brings a hug, information, or compassion to other parts of you. There are so many ways to do this. You can do this inside EMDR reprocessing. You can do this as a form of resourcing.

I want to share a small piece of parts work that my grown-up parts wrote to my middle-school parts. This is a recent piece, having done a lot of my own work, but it models the hug, the self-compassion, the information that kid parts don't have, and the recognition of strength and resilience in surviving at all ages. This piece is inspired by my childhood school pictures, which had long been a source of self-hatred:

For the longest time, you'll see the gap in your teeth big enough to slide the kind of quarter that used to buy something. You'll see the crazy mop that is your hair and you'll humiliate and shame yourself for these things. You'll wish you looked like James, Kevin, or Jerry… all smooth, cut, and slick. With a blue ballpoint pen, you'll etch yourself entirely out of your middle school yearbook.

But, I want you to know that you are going to grow up. You are going to buy new cars and marvelous old houses. You are going to make friends who will see you. You're going to have a child of your own. You're going to learn some things that will help sort out what is yours from what was done to you. You will experience different versions of love.

I look at these pictures and I remember how hard it was to be you and I appreciate the difficulty of that huge smile that projects that you are okay. I admire the creativity of your survival. I want to go back and I want to give you a hug. I want to check in on you, because I know that you are not okay. I want to go back to you in seventh grade and tell you that 1982 is going to feel like it will kill you. And I'll tell you that I know for certain that it will not. It is going to take a long time and a lot of healing, but you're going to be healthy enough to look at those pictures and love yourself deeply, think that you have always been creative and handsome and that they are all absolutely lovely. They document what was hard. They also document what has always been remarkable. And look, we have still have them.

There were times, not too terribly long ago, when these pictures would have been evidence of defectiveness. Some of the most grown-up parts of me were still carrying the old survival strategies of self-blame and self-flagellation. In order to heal, I needed to have experiences that were different from the expectation in the bad memory. My very first experience in therapy was when I was 24 years old, I needed to have the experience of finding the right adult words to simply describe what I had been through. My first therapist didn't know how to fix it. But she knew how to attune and how to listen.

I had the experience of being with my trauma and also being okay. I had other experiences in love and nurture that were helpful, parts-wise. I had the experience of raising a child and seeing first-hand the needs that a child is born into, and I got the actual experience of providing concrete nurture to something. Later, I had really good therapy. I got to witness people experience really good therapy. As a therapist, I saw people bringing comfort, empathy, and information across parts and across developmental eras. Some of my early clients modeled the work of self-compassion that I had yet to do in myself. After that, I had more good therapy where wounds carried by parts of me were metabolized into the parts of me that already knew that I was already okay.

There are a thousand ways to do parts work well. But EMDR therapy is almost always about connecting information held by parts in particular developmental eras to other parts that are hopefully resourced enough to metabolize that wounding. When the right-now parts aren't healthy enough to metabolize the wounding, or when the younger parts are too stuck, frozen, or existentially lonely, we may need to promote experiences in which parts can connect with other parts in ways that are different from the expectations in the bad memories. Through these experiences, we can create the possibility of what didn't happen. When clients are confused about human needs and whose job it is to meet then, we may need to help them have experiences of getting a need met in imaginal space before it can happen in the system spontaneously. Parts work is about connecting different developmental eras and different parts of the brain, and all of it is done experientially. We are wounded through experiences, and we heal by having different experiences. Parts work can create little pathways, then little roads, then bigger roads, then highways, and then interstates wide enough for self-compassion, self-comprehension, and ultimately self-healing.

There are many approaches to parts work. Many EMDR therapists find utility in the following resources: Internal Family Systems (Schwartz, R. C., & Sweezy, M. 2020), Developmental Needs Meeting Strategy (Schmidt, 2009), Robin Shapiro's Easy Ego State Interventions (Shapiro, 2016), Amy Wagner's The Soul of Dissociation training (JoyfulBrainInstitute.com), Jamie Marich's *Dissociation Made Simple* (2023), and Resource Therapy (ResourceTherapyInternational.com).

Chapter 15
"Mindfulness Doesn't Work for Me:" Teaching it Differently

Many clients with complex trauma will come to us convinced that they have already failed mindfulness and that they are about to fail EMDR therapy. Some of the approaches that I have seen to teaching mindfulness to clients assume that we are working with a client's nervous system that is not pervasively traumatized. Many approaches throw the client into the deep end of the present, the body, or noticing without much preparation or guidance, almost as though they are running every client through the same mindfulness machine. How we approach a client system with severe trauma needs to be different from how we approach a system that is relatively healthy. Our interventions should match the unique nervous system of the client we are working with. So, maybe the problem isn't that many clients simply can't do mindfulness. Maybe they can't do it the way we have been teaching it.

Complex trauma is not a special case. It's nearly the only case we see in community mental health contexts globally. A large percentage of pervasively traumatized clients struggle with even the most basic forms of mindfulness for reasons that we will explore, but also because of how we teach it. The easiest thing to change in this equation is how we teach it. Even in EMDR therapy, we often use language similar to the following: "Ok, now we're in Phase Two, and I'm going to teach you these resources so that you can calm down when you get activated." While the statement is true, do you hear the therapist's agenda in the way we may be introducing it? As you will see, when we are working with clients with extreme trauma what we are looking for is information about the client's nervous system and not necessarily the relaxation response immediately. I want to show you how to use the information that surfaces in the service of the client's recovery.

Moving Against Long-Held Survival Strategies

It is helpful to understand why the tasks of mindfulness are so difficult for clients with complex trauma. We are asking them to move in ways that conflict with long-held survival strategies. We are asking them to do something that their nervous systems have already clearly identified as not safe. If we are going to try to make these mindful tasks safe, we have to see and appreciate the unsafety first.

The Present

Related to what might go wrong, let's think about how many clients with complex trauma are currently surviving. Many clients with complex trauma have problematic relationships with the present, and mindfulness is centered on the present. Many clients have survived by staying ahead of it… whatever it is. Slowing down makes them more anxious. The present is where everything bad happened. Many clients with complex trauma live in an aggregated mashup of the past and the future, neither of which are okay… in fact, they are pretty horrible. This lets you know how horrible the present must feel if that's what they do to avoid it. Things catching up are worse. Slowing down, boredom, or resting may cause things to seep. Clients intuit, often correctly, that slowing down can cause everything they ever pushed aside to show up all at once.

Bodies

A lot of mindfulness is about the experience of the body in the present. The body is where everything bad happened. Just as important, the body is also where very little good happens, including positive affect. Any wisdom of the body was abandoned long ago. A large chunk of dissociation is often of the somatic kind. Approaching the body is a lot like approaching a Korean demilitarized zone; you have to watch where you step and how you move. We'll explore more about that in subsequent chapters.

Noticing

We live in pervasively dissociated cultures. Once we come to see dissociation, we see it everywhere, and it seems like the whole point of Western civilization is to pervasively distract ourselves from ourselves. Culturally, we would do almost anything not to notice and be present with ourselves. How many addictions are to numb our noticing? And once we learn how to not notice, there is almost nothing we can't endure.

Often, clients with severe trauma arrive at a strong motivation to change because something has tripped them (a health issue, a work issue, a relationship issue, or a death) that makes it impossible for them to have the same disconnected relationship with the present and their bodies, and things are happening way above their capacity to ignore. Complex trauma clients in crisis are in a double catastrophe. They are carrying all of their trauma (some of it loose in awareness), and their regular survival strategies aren't working. This is a remarkably difficult time to learn new skills, kind of like trying to learn deep breathing while you are downing or in the middle of a house fire.

The Mind Is Taxed with Survival Tasks

Also in this context, the minds of our clients in crisis are running like jet engines. To be more specific, parts of clients are very active and may be in active conflict with other parts over what to do, what sense to make of, and how to best manage the current catastrophe. Imagine a therapist entering into this dynamic asking the client to slow down and notice, sometimes for long periods at a time, when the mind is at war with itself. Or imagine the mind running like a jet engine and then you ask the client to build the calm scene of a beach. Imagine the difficulty of making the sand, sky, clouds, sunshine, birds, ocean, waves, buildings, and all of the sensory components of that when internally the client's nervous system feels like it's in the Battle of the Bulge. All of these creative tasks are hard to create and tolerate in fight, flight, or freeze.

There Is Performance Anxiety in What They Know We Are About to Ask

Add to all of these things the performance anxiety of trying a skill focused on these places of discomfort and knowing that the therapist is going to ask them about their experience with it. These are clients that are accustomed to being what other people need them to be, and performance anxiety is associated with "Is this working?" "Am I doing this right?" "What does it mean that I don't find this relaxing?"

Suggestions for Navigating Phase Two Challenges

Step One: Normalize the Difficulties

Normalize the difficulty using all of the information above and all of the information you have learned about the client's survival. You know how to do that. Do it. "Of course mindfulness and the way we have been approaching it hasn't worked well for you. Would you be interested in trying this differently?"

Step Two: Appreciate the Role of Parts and Get Consent

If you are working with a system of parts (and you're always working with a system), get consent from all parts of the system to engage in mindfulness exercises and explain clearly what you are doing differently this time than in the times that didn't work. When parts don't have the opportunity to consent or express concerns, they may communicate their concerns in ways that are likely to be heard and in ways that we used to call "resistance" before we were trauma-focused. This is what one example of asking for consent might look like: "I'd like to teach you a way to notice breathing that doesn't involve taking really deep or slow breaths and doesn't involve noticing the breath in an internal way at all. Is that something that we can try? Does any part of you think that is a bad idea?" If there are concerns, normalize those. Reevaluate if that normalization has resolved the concern for that part. If not, move on for now. That part needs to be heard when it says no.

Step Three: Decrease Exposure Time to the Resource

One of the things that is most triggering to severely traumatized clients is when they get thrown into the deep end of the present, the body, or noticing without any clear instruction about what they are supposed to do or when the exercise will end. It is very important to communicate a task and communicate that each component of this exercise will only last a moment. We don't just communicate that the exercise will be brief; we want to actually guide the client through it very, very briefly, minimize talking, and have the noticing components only last a few seconds.

Step Four: We're Not Necessarily Looking for Something That Is Calming

When working with clients with complex trauma, I'm not necessarily looking for a resource to be calming immediately. It is okay if it is neutral. Many clients say that mindfulness resources make their stress and distress worse. I'm happy if we can find a way to take a breath, to notice distress or pleasure, observe the body, or observe the present without anything getting worse. We can put a toe there. Next session, we can put two toes there. Before long, we will have somewhere for the client to stand. We are looking to create an experience that disconfirms the expectation in the exercise... then we leverage that new learning.

"I can slow down, and a catastrophe doesn't happen."

"I can notice aspects of the internal experience of my body, and a catastrophe doesn't happen."

"I can imagine, very briefly, my younger self getting a hug from an attachment figure resource, and a catastrophe doesn't happen."

For complex trauma clients with very high anxiety, we don't want something that relaxes them a lot quickly. Again, their baseline anxiety is likely a function of the current dysfunction of their parts, and it exists with the intention of keeping the client safe. If clients relax too much, for example, going from an 8/10 distress to a 5/10 distress in a few moments, that's way too deep of a dive with many complex trauma clients. We might expect a counter-reaction to that level of relaxation that may push them far above their baseline nearing panic. Again, the very high anxiety that clients feel is their nervous system attempting to keep them safe. We need to introduce disconfirming information slowly, spread out, and in ways that the system finds tolerable so that the nervous system can more reliably construct predictions and realities that better match the actual present risk.

Step Five: Recalibrate What "Working for Me" Means

Part of what is difficult with mindfulness with many clients who have been in therapy for years may be how prior therapists have taught mindfulness with an agenda. Again, what I'm looking for is information. Whatever we get, whatever happens, it's just information, and we will use that information to inform what comes next in the service of the client's recovery.

We need to redefine what "working for me" means with someone who is hypervigilant and on the edge of panic. Few people have the ability to go from an 8/10 level of stress to relaxed. What they may be able to do is to briefly tap the break and go from an 8/10 stress to 7/10 stress in some place in their body. After a few minutes, the body returns to an 8/10 level. That is what "working for you" means with clients with severe trauma-related stress. And we need to recalibrate that as success. If had a headache and you gave me an aspirin and it only helped for 10 seconds, I would say with an absolutely straight face that the aspirin "didn't work for me." But when we first approach a pervasively traumatized nervous system, that is what "working for me" means. We need to normalize that.

Imagine two cars. One represents a non-traumatized nervous system that is simply coasting at 45 miles per hour. What happens when you tap the brake pedal? The car slows down, sometimes dramatically, until something happens that pushes the gas pedal. The other car represents a pervasively traumatized nervous system. It's a car with a cinderblock on the gas pedal and moves at 95 miles per hour. What happens when you tap the brake? If it slows at all, it slows down a little. As soon as you take your foot off the brake, it returns to 95 miles per hour. This is normal. The problem is how the cinderblock on the gas pedal changes what normal looks like. We need to teach clients how to tap the brake despite it not "working" deeply and immediately. We need teach them first how to tap the brake at all and ask them to observe that a catastrophe didn't happen. If we tap the brake and anxiety does get worse, we need to normalize how hard the client parts are working to keep him safe. If our parts don't trust tapping the brake, then we need to engage those parts when we touch the brake even lighter and for even less time.

Step Six: Bridge Resources

Once we understand the client's nervous system a little bit better and it becomes clearer how and where their system is protecting them, we can start to construct bridges. When clients attempt resources, but they don't make it to the other side, we need to construct bridge resources. Bridge or Dip Your Toe In resources have built-in accommodations at the very places where many clients with complex trauma struggle. When clients struggle to visualize, refer to other chapters in this section of the book to show you how to outsource the visualization components to YouTube or other video services. Once clients have bridge resources, we have a place to put a toe. We can leverage that until we have a place for a foot. They can breathe deeper with that footing, explore the calm scene using all of their senses, and dip their toes into the present a little more fully from that place.

Step Seven: Externalize Noticing and Make It Concrete

Many mindfulness resources are far too spacious and abstract. Many of the bridge resources in the chapters below direct the client to notice very specific and concrete things. The grounding exercises direct clients to notice sensory elements specifically using temperature, color, texture, etc. The breathing exercises externalize the breath and ask the client to visualize the breath or notice sensory elements of the breath in externalized and concrete ways. The body scan exercise asks clients to touch their own bodies and get information from both their hands and the part of the body that they are evaluating.

Step Eight: Send Clients Home to Practice at Their Baseline, Not When Triggered

Another missed opportunity in how we typically teach mindfulness is that we teach these tentative resources in session, and then we send clients home to practice them only when they are absolutely losing their minds. If I gave you key lime pie to eat only when you are on the edge of panic, how long before the smell of key lime pie will cause a panic attack? Again, we are looking for disconfirming information. Leveraging that disconfirming information is how we will help clients lower their baseline anxiety. Tap the brake briefly and observe that nothing bad happened. Tap the brake, and notice that nothing bad happened. Tap the brake, notice that it may calm you a little bit, and nothing bad happens. What we are dipping our toes in is lower distress and learning that lower distress can also feel safe enough. This can create the possibility of the client's parts relaxing or at least seeing some advantage in trying the exercise. If we only do this when something has triggered us, we don't actually dip down into the disconfirming information. Long story short, let the nervous system realize that tapping the brake can be safe. Let it learn that this is one of the things we do when we are trying to calm down. Do this at the client's baseline. If you do, within a few weeks, it may be available when the client really needs it.

Putting It All Together

Start by normalizing the idea that the nervous system is trying to provide for the client's safety because it doesn't know that it has survived what it has survived. Ask permission from the client's system to try something different and briefly dip a toe into disconfirming information. Normalize that we're not necessarily looking for something to dramatically calm you right out of the gate, and recalibrate what a resource working for you means, given your current system state. Construct bridges when the client jumps but doesn't arrive on the other side of the resource. Finally, practice these resources at your baseline until your system identifies them as safe.

While there are a lot of other ways to do the same types of things, what we don't want to do is simply pronounce that the client isn't ready. We need to meet them where they are with modifications and accommodations. Otherwise, the client will die not ready. When our intention is to do EMDR therapy, we need to identify the difficulties and work on them every session and between sessions until they are prepared enough for trauma reprocessing.

Chapter 16
Why Attachment Resources Are Often Needed

EMDR therapy allows old stuck information to connect to and metabolize into existing adaptive information. If there is any magic in EMDR therapy, it is in the speed and depth of the complete transformation of stuck information into adaptive information. As we have seen elsewhere in this book, Shapiro is clear that there must be enough of the needed adaptive information for the difficult information to connect to and be metabolized into (thus the Boat and the Whale metaphor, the Mount Everest metaphor, the Marathon metaphor, and others).

How do people develop adaptive information? We develop it by having learning experiences that are different from the learning that occurred in the trauma. We develop it the same way that we heal from trauma, by having experiences that disconfirm the expectation in the bad memories. An excellent way to develop a large amount of adaptive information is to have a great life that includes a protected and attuned childhood. Absent that, we need to get it somewhere. It is entirely possible that many clients with complex trauma will have never had experiences where they felt protected, where they were able to express needs and get them met, where self-compassion was promoted, and where appropriate roles were modeled. Many people that we work with are fully grown adults who hold many of the same beliefs about themselves, about their traumas, and about the world that they held when they were young children. All parts of them believe all the same lies. These are remarkably difficult case presentations for a psychotherapy that depends entirely on your parts system holding somewhere in it enough of the disconfirming information to unlock the trauma. In short, some part of you must already hold the right answer for you to unlock trauma and heal in EMDR therapy. When no part of you does, we need to construct experiences that generate and strengthen this information.

Psychoeducation can play an important role, but when it comes to corrective information about human needs, clients need to have corrective experiences. We can't quickly and sensibly send a client with a pervasively traumatized nervous system out into the world and expect them to have different or disconfirming experiences with others. If we do, they will interact with others and experience it through their traumatized nervous system and are likely to have experiences that reinforce past wounding.

Parts work can help with the task of developing adaptive information experientially. Parts work is a way for client parts to have relational experiences with other parts that disconfirm the expectations in the bad memory. It's a way for parts to begin the process of self-reconciliation, self-listening, self-development, and self-nurture. Many of the various approaches to parts work can be helpful here. Or, a well-developed and well-practiced attachment figure resource is an expedited way to do parts work that addresses the specific developmental and informational deficits that are relevant to doing EMDR therapy well.

A well-developed attachment figure resource borrows slivers from any actual relational experience of kindness, support, validation, nurture, protection, attunement, or assistance from anyone in any developmental era of the client's life. It can be borrowed from teachers, neighbors, friends, partners, family members, coworkers, or anyone who interacted with the client from a position of genuine care. When the client has deficits of positive experiences, we can borrow from media like movies, books, or television series. When we can't borrow from media, we borrow from imagination.

On the top line, we develop attachment figure resources because we anticipate that clients will get stuck when working on attachment wound memories, and these resources allow us to end sessions in ways that are not horrible. They are a powerful fire extinguisher that puts out the radioactive fire of existential childhood loneliness by bringing the activated child state a hug, nurture, and helpful information.

The attachment figure resource also models for the most resourced parts how to be kind and extend empathy to the activated child parts. The most grown-up parts can witness a kid part getting its needs met, even if in imagination, and the world does not end. When the most grown-up parts observe someone treat their kid parts with kindness and compassion, it is easier for those parts to replicate what was demonstrated to them. Often the attachment figure resource creates the mental construct of self-compassion, which makes it easier for the grown-up parts to subsequently execute. The attachment figure resource initially creates a small deer path between long-estranged and dissociated parts and development eras. Repeated use creates a road, highway, and eventually an interstate wide enough for attachment wounds to transit. A well-developed and well-practiced attachment figure resource may be the first instance for many clients to have concrete experiences of self-compassion and effective self-communication.

We develop an attachment figure resource when the most resourced parts aren't healthy enough, hold strong resentments toward the child states, or lack the adaptive information needed to metabolize the information in the traumatic memory. The attachment figure resources are a proxy or substitute that models what the most grown-up parts can't currently do. As soon as the most resourced parts are healthy enough, we allow the trauma stuck in parts of you to connect to the adaptive information held in other parts of you through EMDR therapy.

As you will see in my attachment figure script in the following chapter, my preference is to put all of the needed qualities into one figure. Other trainers may help clients develop multiple figures where each one brings a specific quality, like protection or nurture. I combine them into one figure because that more closely matches what we actually needed—one person who was able to meet our needs consistently enough. Also, Parnell (2013) and others are fond of developing an Ideal Mother attachment figure resource. My early clients were consistently unable to develop an Ideal Mother attachment figure resource, because imagining a replacement mother triggered memories of their actual mother, the same way that trying to develop an uncle-like attachment figure can be triggering if the client's actual uncle was a monster. Most of my clients develop attachment figures of "a mother" who lives in a house in the neighborhood. Others use a grandfather-like figure or some other relational slot.

We anticipate that the attachment figure resource will be difficult to develop for many clients. For clients who are phobic of attachment or connection, we can try to use the Dip Your Toe In Attachment Figure Resource described in that section of the book. If the client has difficulty, we can always pause and let things settle. We can try resuming it in subsequent sessions. A well-developed attachment figure resource can bring up a substantial amount of grief. If grief appears, help the client identify it as grief and encourage the client to experience it with the expectation that it will move through them like a wave.

As with all resources, encourage the client to practice this resource at their baseline, rather than practicing first during their periods of high distress. Let the resource become identified as something that we do to calm down on purpose in quieter times, before using it as a way to regulate during an emotional catastrophe.

Chapter 17
The Attachment Figure Resource Script

There are many ways to develop and use attachment figure resources in EMDR therapy. This is just one approach. This version guides the client to install nurturing, protective, attunement, and guidance qualities into the attachment figure resource. The advantage of putting everything needed into one imaginary resource is that this method more closely matches what children developmentally need.

Why Some Clients May Need Attachment Figure Resources

EMDR therapy requires that enough adaptive information be present for clients to process old stuck information/trauma. Metaphorically, we cannot land a fish (memory) bigger than our boat (adaptive information). When it comes to adaptive information, clients with complex trauma and attachment wounding typically have small boats. Many clients with attachment wounding have profound deficits in the right-now selves that can make reprocessing difficult. Some of these deficits are judgment or hostility toward the self as a child, difficulties with self-comfort and regulation, pervasive guilt/shame/blame/responsibility for both traumatic events and traumatic neglect, and pervasive internalization of the negative messages from others throughout their lives.

When I refer to the client's "adult parts" throughout the sections on parts work, I mean specifically the most resourced parts. The most resourced parts are often the most adult parts, but not always.

If we struggled to get our needs met when we were young, parts of ourselves may struggle to extend kindness or compassion to other parts of ourselves. This connecting of parts is a key element in healing.

Why Develop an Attachment Figure Resource?

A well-developed and practiced attachment figure resource can do the following:

- Be a powerful resource to help clients regulate between sessions.
- Allow lonely or stuck parts of the client to receive comfort without the client's adult parts having to explicitly provide it (since the adult parts may not be healthy enough or may hold too much judgment to do so).
- Allow the most adult parts to witness (as a rehearsal) the child parts getting comfort and support.
- Address the existential loneliness that defined much of childhood and may have shut down reprocessing.
- Promote easier connection and communication between the current adult selves and child states.
- Let difficult reprocessing sessions end safely (using the fish/boat metaphor above, if we hook an attachment whale that is too big for the boat we have today, the attachment figure is a powerful set of scissors that can allow us to safely and predictably disconnect from it for now).
- Dramatically minimize the risk of decompensation when working on attachment wounds in reprocessing.

We do not develop these imaginary attachment figures to deny any difficult realities of childhood. We develop them so that we can take this healing journey more safely and so that we can consistently end sessions with as little residual distress as possible. Sometimes we may encounter a memory that is larger than we have the resources or time to manage in a session, and a well-developed and practiced attachment figure resource can help settle the big emotions and realities of the childhood memory, letting us continue more easily as adults in the adult world when the session ends.

Assessing for the Need to Use Attachment Figure Resources

Ask the client as part of Phase One in EMDR therapy the following question: *"When you were young, who was really and consistently there for you when you needed help or were upset?"*

Or, ***"When you were young and you were upset, who could reliably and consistently help you feel better about yourself?"***

If the client was not able to identify multiple sources of strong and consistent attachment, consider developing an attachment figure resource. Note that the consistency and accessibility of these people were also important. If the client had a close relationship with a grandmother, but she lived far away, the attachment figure may not have been available *enough* to address the developmental needs of the client as a child. When there are deficits in childhood attachment, we can generally assume that there may be difficulties with the most adult client parts being able to solidly connect with child parts (which may be an essential pathway in client healing).

Developing the Relational Slot (Figure's Relationship to You)

In this approach, the attachment figure is not an actual person. It is imaginary. We can borrow heavily from an actual person and add those qualities to the imaginary figure. Real people are complicated, and we want to keep the complications out. We start by working with the client to define a relational slot (as in, what is this imaginary attachment figure's relationship to you?). This can be a mother-in-the-neighborhood figure, an aunt-like figure, an uncle-like figure, a grandmother-like or grandfather-like figure, a teacher-like figure, or any other person who might have been nice when the client was young.

Considerations to make when selecting the relational slot for the attachment figure:

- It needs to be accessible (we need to be able to imagine it in the neighborhood).
- It needs to live outside of the childhood home (otherwise, it may come in direct conflict with abusers, which may only invite complications). However, it needs to have enough moral authority so that it can come to get you or you can safely go there whenever you like or need to.
- Avoid selecting a relational slot that is the same as an abuser. For example, the idea of an uncle-like figure may be too polluted if the client's uncle was an abuser (simply the word "uncle" can be a trauma trigger). It is often okay for the attachment resource to be

a mom-in-the-neighborhood figure, even if the client's mother was abusive.
- If the client wants to use a sibling-like figure as the attachment figure, try to nudge away from that because this is not developmentally appropriate (because the person who we will be imagining giving you comfort and safety is also a child). If the client insists on using a sibling-like figure, try to make the figure as close to the adult years as possible.
- You can borrow from movies, media, anime, etc. Attachment figures can be cross-gender and even cross-species, but they really need to be something that the client, as a child, would have found nurturing and comforting. Some people want to use Jesus as an attachment resource, but consider if Jesus would have been accessible to the client at six, seven, or eight years old (or may simply be another adult who should be able to provide comfort but isn't present, human, or emotionally accessible enough to).

When you were young, who would have been nice to have in the neighborhood… would have been nice to visit. This can be a grandmother- or grandfather-like figure, an aunt- or uncle-like figure, a teacher-like figure, or just a mom- or a dad-like figure who lives near you and is available to you. This person is imaginary but can borrow qualities from people who you have had at various times in your life who treated you like you were important.

Adding Qualities to the Attachment Figure

Once the relational slot is selected, there are two main pathways we can use to add qualities to the attachment figure: we can borrow qualities from people/experiences that we have had, or we can imagine those qualities. Most well-developed attachment figures borrow some from family members, friends, teachers, or mentors (who were kind and supportive) and are supplemented by imagining some of the remaining qualities. Clients with extensive trauma may not have much adaptive information that we can borrow from memory. In these cases, we are left with imagination, media, movies, etc. When borrowing from actual people, we can modify the questions in the script to: **"How did this person show that they cared about you?"** Slow tap those qualities in. Once we have those qualities installed, use the guide below to imagine the qualities that may be missing. For each of these categories below, there may be multiple aspects or qualities that we can tap into or "soak into" this attachment figure.

Physical Features and Inviting a Quick Hug

Once we have decided on the relational slot, we ask clients to imagine and notice the physicality of a hug. This can be done before we add any emotional or needed qualities so that if there is a problem with the hug, it's easier to figure out now than if we have problems later. We do not specify whether the *you* that is receiving the hug is the adult self or the child self (since introducing child selves at this stage can be triggering… let the client take it where they take it).

Is this person you are imagining tall or short, thin or heavy? I'm asking because I'm about to ask you to imagine a quick hug from someone this size and shape. Before we put any emotional qualities into this figure, can you imagine what it would be like to receive a quick hug from someone like this? Just imagine it for a few seconds…

Good. How was that?

If the client reports a positive or neutral response, you can invite them into about 10 seconds of slow bilateral and notice or soak up that response. If the response was not positive or neutral, normalize that and try to troubleshoot the problem.

Food

Other than with people who have histories of disordered eating, starting with food is a very good and relatively safe place to start.

Is there anything this person would have cooked for you or would have had in the house for you?

Notice that you are in their kitchen while they are cooking x for you.

Good. How was that?

If the client reports a positive or neutral response, you can invite them into about 10 seconds of slow bilateral and notice or **soak up** that response. If the response was not positive or neutral, normalize that and try to troubleshoot the problem.

Play

Play is a central task of childhood. For many people, play was a lonely or complicated activity in childhood, and the opportunity to bring connection and nurture into play can be helpful.

How would this figure play with you? What would they play with you? Can you notice that?

Good. How was that?

If the client reports a positive or neutral response, you can invite them into about 10 seconds of slow bilateral and notice or soak up that response. If the response was not positive or neutral, normalize that and try to troubleshoot the problem.

Attunement/Importance/Nurture

Option 1: *If this person hasn't seen you for a while and you went to their house, how would they greet you?* If positive, invite slow bilateral: *Can you notice that?*

Option 2: *How would this person show you that you were important?* If positive, invite slow bilateral: *Can you notice that?*

Good. How was that? If anything difficult comes up in this step, it is often grief related to what didn't happen. Normalize that. It makes sense that imagining something we did not get may cause us to have an emotional response.

Presence

Simply being in the presence of someone who can "safely" provide nurture, attunement, protection, and information can be calming and help meet developmental needs.

Can you notice what it feels like simply to be in the presence of this person... imagine just sitting in a living room and visiting or watching television? If positive, invite slow bilateral: *Can you notice that?*

Good. How was that? If anything difficult comes up in this step, it is often grief related to what didn't happen. Normalize that. It makes sense that imagining something we did not get may cause us to have an emotional response.

Safety/Protection

Try to avoid directly triggering the trauma that may have happened from parents or the childhood home. It may be a gentler approach to imagine the attachment figure providing some safety and protection using children in the neighborhood.

What would this person do if a kid in the neighborhood was being mean to another kid or said something unkind? If positive, invite slow bilateral: *Can you notice that?*

Good. How was that? If anything difficult comes up in this step, it is often grief related to the protection that didn't happen that should have. Normalize that as grief when appropriate. It makes sense that imagining something we did not get may cause us to have an emotional response.

Guidance

It is difficult to trust that people who do not know how to nurture us are able to provide accurate guidance about how to navigate the world. One of the key things attachment figures provide are suggestions for how to manage difficulties in the world.

If you were encountering difficulties at school or with friends, how would this person be able to help you figure out these problems? If positive, invite slow bilateral: *Can you notice that?*

Good. How was that? If anything difficult comes up in this step, it is often grief related to the guidance that didn't happen that should have. Normalize that as grief when appropriate. It makes sense that imagining something we did not get may cause us to have an emotional response.

Other Things

Is there anything else that this person needs to have that may have been helpful to us when we were young?

If positive, invite slow bilateral: *Can you notice that?*

Good. How was that? If anything difficult comes up in this step, it is often grief related to the things that didn't happen that should have. Normalize that as grief when appropriate. It makes sense that imagining something we did not get may cause us to have an emotional response.

Homework

A well-developed attachment figure is also a well-practiced attachment figure. We do not want the first time the client relies on the attachment figure to be inside a difficult EMDR therapy reprocessing session. We want to invite the client to use the attachment figure resource often between sessions.

Now that you have this attachment figure, please use [him/her/them] between sessions when you need comfort or information. Bringing this attachment figure in between sessions is an important part of using it successfully when we need to in sessions.

Common Problems or Possible Complications

People with pervasive trauma may have pervasive deficits in attachment and may have very little adaptive information that we can borrow. This is okay but introduces some potential complications. We can also borrow from movies, books, superheroes, comics, or characters from television series. We borrow from wherever we can.

One of the most common obstacles in the development of an attachment figure resource is the sudden emergence of grief related to childhood needs that were not met. Grief makes sense. Normalize it. If the grief process is too strong to continue, even after normalizing it, we can split the development of the attachment figure into multiple sessions.

Additional Resources

Much of the early and important work and training at the intersection of EMDR therapy and attachment resources was done by Laurel Parnell (2013), who continues to train. This script is heavily informed by Parnell's work. More recently, other approaches to working with parts can accomplish many of the same goals and can address similar deficits.

Chapter 18
Introducing Fire Extinguisher Resources Early

Clients with complex trauma often present on fire with one or more significant trauma symptoms. As soon as possible, I will introduce some of the core resources that we will use throughout therapy. Helping clients with resources to manage current somatic catastrophes (panic attacks, flashbacks, trauma-related dreams, etc.) are excellent interventions that also help demonstrate therapist competence with trauma and help build/support the initial therapist-client relationship. These resources are selected and introduced based on the client's current symptomology. I may introduce these resources prior to discussing EMDR therapy and I may introduce some of them as soon as the first session.

Initial Resources Without Bilateral Stimulation

When I first introduce the initial resources in the first or second session, I do not invite the client to engage in any form of left-right stimulation. Many clients with complex trauma have struggled with many forms of mindfulness exercises, and I'm careful not to add anything that may complicate the resource. In fact, I go out of my way to make the resource simpler, more concrete, and much faster. The bilateral stimulation (BLS) is among the most culturally bizarre aspects of EMDR therapy, and it is often sensible to develop the resource without adding BLS if preparation is likely to take months. It is easy to add slow BLS to the resource once it is identified as safe by the client's nervous system and once the client is prepared for the processing phases. My initial goal in these resources is to help the client manage a current difficult symptom for the purpose of supporting current stability.

What's Different in the Dip Your Toe In Resources

The Dip Your Toe in Resources share many of the modifications and accommodations to more standard mindfulness resources discussed in the prior chapter. They are summarized as follows:

- Assume that difficulties may arise. If they do, normalize and try to troubleshoot them. If needed, disengage from the resource, come back to it later, and dip your toe into it even faster next time.
- Describe the resource and ask for consent from all of the client's parts. If the client has reservations, I'd like to explore those concerns as soon as possible and not have them show up in the resource as a surprise.
- Engage in the resource very, very briefly at first. Generally, each resource should be fully completed in under 45 seconds total. You can always add time and make it more spacious once the client's nervous system is able to settle using it. If stretching it out causes anxiety to appear, shorten it and stay there for a while.
- When first approaching a resource, clients expect that the resource will make things worse. We are looking for a way to do it that does not make anything worse.
- Calibrate success as being able to do the resource in ways that do not make anxiety worse. We can leverage that. If a relaxation response appears, expect that the client will return to baseline anxiety within a few moments. Normalize that.
- Make the object of noticing concrete and externalize it when possible.
- Ask the client to practice the resource between sessions several times a day at their baseline for at least a few days, until the resource is solidly identified by the client's nervous system as a good idea.

You can do these resources with your clients, and they will not always "work." This is not your fault. This is a more sensible and sensitive way to introduce resources to clients with complex trauma, but this work is always difficult and is often highly non-intuitive for their nervous systems. Still, in this complex dynamic of trying to resource pervasively traumatized clients, the easiest thing to change is how we approach the client's nervous system. You will get information. That information will come as a gift in the service of the client's recovery. Figuring out what to do with this information is the real art and the real intuition of learning to do this work well.

Chapter 19
Dip Your Toe In Sensory Grounding Script

A lot of what is difficult about trauma is the way that the past or future worries show up in the present. The ability to find your way back to the present, to this current moment, is a valuable resource. Even if things in the present aren't necessarily where we would like them to be or where they need to be, the present moment probably is safer than the worst parts of a bad memory or the worst parts of a future worry. The present is where we actually are, and it's the only place where we can take actual and specific actions to keep ourselves safe if we need to.

The goal of this exercise is simply to help develop the ability to be more present when you want to be or when you need to be.

In this exercise, I will ask you to check your senses one at a time very quickly, typically for just a few seconds each. I won't ask you anything about it until the end, and I don't need or expect you to have any specific response to this exercise. The whole exercise should be over in about 45 seconds. Does this sound like something that all parts of you are willing to quickly try? We can stop at any time and for any reason.

Before starting, see if the client can source something for the sense of smell (candle, essential oil, drink, ChapStick, etc.) and for the sense of taste (drink, piece of candy, etc.). For each of the questions below, the client does not need to answer you out loud; they just need to explore and notice the answer internally. If they would like, they can speak the answer.

Look around your current room and notice several things that you see, the color or colors of each object, and notice that if you were to touch it would it be hard, soft, or some other texture? [Wait four seconds.] **Good.**

If there is a piece of furniture near you, place a hand on it and notice if it is warmer, cooler, or the same temperature as your hand. [Wait 2 seconds.] *As you move your hand across that object, is it completely smooth or do you notice a texture?* [Wait two seconds.]

I'm going to be really quiet, Just notice what you hear in order of loudest first. [Wait four seconds.]

If you have something near you that has a smell, just engage with that smell. [Wait four seconds.]

If you have something near you that has a taste, just taste it and notice the taste. [Wait four seconds.]

How did that go? Did it make anything worse? Did that resource let you feel any more connected to this current room? [If not, that's okay, normalize that.]

If the client reports a generally positive or neutral response: ***Good. Which of the senses seemed the most helpful in connecting you to the present moment and this current room?***

Notes:

- Normalize any difficulties.
- The goal of this resource is to promote very brief grounding in the present. Grounding can serve as a powerful containment exercise for rumination and can be a core element in stopping flashbacks once they start.
- Encourage the client to do grounding often when needed, but have the client practice it between sessions for several days at baseline levels of stress so that it is rugged enough to be used when really needed.

Chapter 20
Dip Your Toe In Grounding for Flashbacks Script

This resource is taught to clients who have frequent flashbacks, and it is taught immediately after the Dip Your Toe In Sensory Grounding resource.

This exercise involves using a photo to help you stop a flashback once it starts. Can you find a photo on the internet (or in a magazine) that is colorful and also feels relaxing? For instance, if it is an ocean scene, I might invite you to notice all the colors of blue in the ocean as they move from dark blue to white as the waves are on the beach. Are all parts of you willing to try this with me? [Allow them to try to find one that works.]

Can you describe the photo for me? Are there any color shifts in the photo that you can notice deeply (for instance, shifts in the blue of the ocean that I just described)? Can you notice deeply the changes and shifts in colors, as though you are trying to see every version of that color? [pause] *I am asking you to try this to saturate the color-perceiving parts of your brain in order to push aside any visual elements of the flashback.*

As soon as you notice that you are having a flashback, I'd like you to stare deeply at this photo. Can you find a place to store it where you can access it quickly? Try to notice every shift of the color you have identified in it. Try to notice the colors in the photo until the only thing you see is the photo. We use the photo as a kind of bridge to help your brain focus first on a visual object that is in your hand. When the only thing that you see is the colors in the photo, put the photo down and do the sensory grounding that we just explored.

Look around your current room and notice whatever you see and notice the color attached to the object. Say things out loud, like "those are my shoes" *to help anchor you in your current room and the present time.*

Touch a piece of furniture near you and notice its temperature from the perspective of warmer, cooler, or the same temperature as your hand.

Notice whatever you hear in order of loudest first.

Find something to smell and notice that.

Find (or go get) something to taste and notice that.

Make at least a small change to your immediate environment. For instance, if you had been sitting, move. If you had been standing, sit for a moment.

Notes:

- Normalize any difficulties. Expect that it may not work at all the first few times the client tries it. Keep trying it.
- The goal of this resource is to stop a flashback once it starts. It will not stop them from happening but can dramatically shorten the activation when they occur.
- It may not be accompanied by an immediate relaxation response.
- Encourage the client to do grounding often when needed, but have the client practice it between sessions for several days at baseline levels of stress so that it is rugged enough to be used when really needed.
- As with all of the Dip Your Toe In resources, there is no left-right stimulation utilized we add it just prior to going to the processing phases.

Chapter 21
Dip Your Toe In Body Scan Script

In this exercise, I encourage the therapist to use their hands on their own bodies to model the checking we are asking the client to do. This is a very quick exercise. You will be checking each place for only a few seconds.

In this resource, we use our hands to briefly check on the experience of our bodies in the present. I'll do this exercise with you and check on the experience of my own body in the present. We will just quickly check the speed of our thoughts as well as the tightness of our jaw, neck, and shoulder muscles. We will also check the chest, central body, and stomach areas for any stress or other sensations. We will only check each place for a few seconds, and whatever you notice or don't notice is fine. This entire exercise should be over in less than 45 seconds. We can stop anytime you like. Do all parts of you think trying this exercise is an okay thing to do right now?

Very quickly, put a hand on each side of the top of your head. How fast are your thoughts running in this moment? You don't need to tell me; just notice. Good.

Using information from your fingertips and from your jaw muscles, touch your jaw muscles and notice if they are soft like a pillow or tight like a steel cable. A pillow is a zero, a steel cable is a ten. Give it a quick number, and don't overthink it. Good.

Same thing with your neck muscles; just reach around and check from zero to ten. Good.

Now, the muscles on the top of your shoulders. Quickly check from zero to ten. Good.

Place a hand over the center of your chest. Do you notice a knot, pressure, tension, heaviness, emptiness, movement, or upset? If so, identify which and give it a number zero to ten. Good.

Place a hand between your chest and your stomach, where your ribs come together. Again, do you notice a knot, pressure, tension, heaviness, emptiness, movement, or upset? If so, identify which and give it a number zero to ten. Good.

Now, check your stomach. Is there a knot, pressure, tension, heaviness, emptiness, movement, or upset. If so, identify which and give it a number zero to ten. Good.

Have a conversation when done with this resource about what they noticed. If the client presents with complaints of severe anxiety and panic, yet has zeros below the jaw, that may indicate some somatic disconnection or dissociation. This is one of the most helpful resources to assess for embodiment. You should not assume that clients with complex trauma are in their bodies enough to notice. If they are not, we need to try to get them embodied enough to notice and that can take time. I typically do this by pairing this resource with other resources.

Notes:

- The purpose of this resource is to quickly assess for embodiment today. Results may vary based on the client's current emotional state and current window of tolerance. Don't assume that difficulty accessing baseline stress in the body today means that this is always the case for this client. Have a conversation about awareness and where the client usually notices distress or stress.
- Do not mistake the fact that a client has panic attacks as evidence that they are embodied enough to do EMDR therapy.
- If we are going to be asking the client to notice for 45 minutes at a time in EMDR therapy and notice things that may be very distressing, we need to test the client's capacity to notice.

Chapter 22
Dip Your Toe In Calm Scene Script

This resource invites us to find a relaxing, distracting, or funny video on YouTube to use as a calm scene. Some people find that videos of relaxing scenes are easier to get in touch with than imaginary ones. Would all parts of you be willing to work with me to find a scene that can help shift mood at least a little bit in the present moment? What kinds of things do you love or find funny or amusing?

Work with the client to find an appropriate video. Suggestions for search terms: beach island waves, cooking shows, dogs catching balls, funny things kids say, campfire meditation, kittens wrestling, etc.

If the scene is relaxing to the client, have them watch several minutes of it to make sure that it works. Then guide the client to do something like the following: **As best you can, try to imagine yourself there. Notice whatever you would be seeing in that scene. Notice what you would be hearing, smelling, or feeling in that scene.**

If the scene is not relaxing, but funny or distracting, have them watch several minutes of it to make sure that it works. Then guide the client to do the following: **As best you can, just notice what is happening in the scene. Observe your response to watching this scene.**

Notes:

- The purpose of this resource is to find a scene that the client can dissociate into that shifts mood at least a little bit in the present.
- The advantage of outsourcing the calm scene to a video is that it works well for clients who have very active minds and overthink constructing an imaginary calm scene or for people who struggle with visualizing.

- Don't worry that the calm scene video may not seem as accessible as an imaginary one. Phones are often closer and more accessible to clients than anything else in their lives.

Chapter 23
Dip Your Toe In Blue Smoke Breathing Script

Sometimes people struggle with breathing exercises because these exercises feel too slow, they do not notice a relaxation response during or after, or because they are unsure what they are supposed to be doing during the exercise. In this exercise, I will ask you to take one breath with me. This breath does not need to be deep or slow.

On the out-breath, I will ask you to try to imagine the breath as colored smoke. Do all parts of you think that trying one breath with me is an okay thing to do? Good.

What color will you try to make the smoke? Good.

Whenever you are ready, take a breath at a rate that is comfortable. Again, it doesn't have to be deep or slow and just try to visualize your out-breath.

How did that go? Did that make anything worse?

If the breath was an okay experience, try another. I typically do not ask the client to do more than three breaths total. If the client notices a small relaxation response, normalize that as success and anticipate that it is about to return to baseline in a few moments.

Notes:

- The purpose of this breath is to find a disconfirming way to breathe and hopefully to avoid anything getting worse. This is particularly true when deep breathing has always caused an anxiety response.
- The purpose is not to generate a strong relaxation response, since that may not be identified by the client's system as safe. We are

just briefly tapping the brake and noticing that it does not make things worse or that it causes a brief and mild relaxation response.
- If clients struggle with this breath, try hand breathing later (next chapter). Hand breathing is generally better tolerated.
- As a modification to this breath, you can ask the client to quickly check the pace of their thoughts while she is visualizing the blue smoke. We are asking the client to visually construct their out-breath, and this often takes the parts of the brain needed to ruminate offline. This breath has the side-benefit of sometimes slowing the pace of thoughts on the out-breath.

Chapter 24
Dip Your Toe In: Hand Breathing Script

In this breath exercise, I will invite you to take a single breath on your hand about a foot away from your mouth and first notice the temperature of the out-breath on your hand. Breathing this way gives you something to notice that is outside of you. Are all parts of you willing to try this single breath with me?

Okay, on the out-breath, breathe in any way that is comfortable (it does not have to be deep or long) on your hand, and notice if the breath feels warmer, cooler, or the same temperature as your hand. Good.

If that was okay, I invite you on the next breath to notice where the breath is hitting your hand. Do you most notice it in specific places, or do you notice it everywhere? Try to visualize where the air is hitting your hand. Good.

If that was okay, I invite you on the next breath to notice how the air is interacting with your hand. Notice how it bounces off your hand in some places and moves through your fingers in other places. Try to visualize how the air is interacting with your hand. Good. What are you noticing?

Notes:

- The purpose of this breath is to find a disconfirming way to breathe and hopefully avoid anything getting worse.
- The purpose is not to generate a strong relaxation response, since that may not be identified by the client's system as safe. We are just briefly tapping the brake and noticing that it does not make things worse or that it causes a brief and mild relaxation response.
- If clients struggle with this breath, pause and try another time.

Chapter 25
A Dip Your Toe In Attachment Figure Resource

The Dip Your Toe In attachment figure resource is a slight modification to the standard attachment figure script in an earlier chapter. If the client struggles using the attachment script, a way to try the resource on is to develop the attachment resource for a kid who is not you when you were young. It can be for a random kid in a park or a child in the client's apartment complex. It is important that the resource not be developed for one of the children of the client (since that may bring up complicated parenting issues). Developing this figure for a child who is not the client helps get around some of the initial self-hatred and blame that automatically appears when many adults with complex trauma think of themselves as children.

Because I anticipate that there will be challenges in developing this Dip Your Toe In attachment figure, do not add slow BLS as indicated in the script in the prior chapter. Slow BLS can be added when the client is closer to the processing phases (which will likely be many sessions away).

If the client is able to develop an attachment figure resource for a child who is not himself, it may be easier for the client to develop one later that is himself. Once the resource for a child who is not the client is installed in the nervous system, we may ask: "If we were going to develop an attachment resource for you, which qualities feel most tolerable to borrow from that resource we developed for that kid who is not you?"

Chapter 26
More About Consent from Parts

The more complex the trauma is in early childhood, the more likely that clients will have a system of parts that present in ways that will need focus and attention in the client's recovery. Getting consent from all parts prior to using a resource, reprocessing a target memory, or moving in a therapeutic direction is incredibly helpful. Getting consent gives the client parts an opportunity to speak and express worries. Those concerns are important. It is often better to attempt to address any concerns of a part prior to starting a task, than in the middle of it. Asking for consent gives me a chance to get to know parts and gives them a chance to get to know me. Inquiry allows parts to come to understand that I care about what parts think and what their concerns are. One of my assumptions about trauma is that a lot of the trauma was done to them. We do not approach therapy as something that we do to them. Consent allows parts to consult and collaborate in all aspects of the client's recovery, allowing the client to have the disconfirming experiences of voice, agency, evaluation, and consent.

Some trauma therapists approach consent with client parts as a way to sneak compliance from the client's parts for an intervention that the therapist would like to do to the client. I view consent as a way to gain vital information from the client's system before, during, or after the client experiences the intervention.

Chapter 27
Where the Standard EMDR Resources Tend to Go Bad and How to Fix Them

There is nothing special about Shapiro's preferred resources. They were just her preferred resources. Some of the most powerful resources I have seen clients develop are strengthening the memory of rocking a baby, the memory of petting a dog, the memory of getting a hug from someone safe, or imagining walking on your favorite stretch of trail. Often it is more elegant to leverage and strengthen what the client already has than to introduce something completely new, especially on the first few contacts.

All three of the resources discussed below are primarily visualization resources. Clients who struggle to visualize are very likely to struggle with all three of them. When clients struggle with resources because of difficulties visualizing, try to make the resource more concrete. We can do this by outsourcing the calm scene to a YouTube video (see the section on Dip Your Toe In Calm Scene), showing the clients videos of boxes or empty safes for containers, and asking clients to connect with the somatic memory of being in the sunshine for the light stream resource. Or try other creative ways of making abstract visualizations more concrete.

Calm Scene Exercise

When Abusers Appear

The most common way that a calm scene "goes bad" is when an abuser intrudes into the calm scene. It makes sense that this would happen. Typically we develop the calm scene after we have given psychoeducation about EMDR therapy, which the client will understand clearly as a trauma treatment. The client's nervous system knows that we are doing a calm scene in preparation for doing trauma work. However, we are asking clients not to think about anything difficult. We are about to do trauma work, but don't think about anything difficult. What do parts of the nervous system often want to do? They want to jump ahead to the trauma.

When a resource goes bad, I will try one time and very quickly to salvage it. If that doesn't work, we immediately pivot to grounding or another resource. Abusers showing up in the calm scene are best conceptualized as an intrusive trauma symptom, and these are best addressed by grounding. The time to teach grounding is before you need it, not during a flashback-like experience.

When Grief Appears

Clients often have few experiences with safety and sometimes grandparents or related figures may have had houses or yards that were experienced as somewhat safe in the client's childhood. Clients may be able to connect to these spaces, but they may soon realize the unprocessed grief related to the death of one or both grandparents. It is generally a good idea to assess for unprocessed grief prior to starting a resource where the people associated with the resource have died. Using resources that clients have a deep somatic connection to can be very powerful, we just need to weigh whether the advantages offset the disadvantages. The best practice is to check.

When the Calm Scene Inadvertently Connects to Trauma

Some of the most powerful calm scene resources connect to existing somatic connections and memories of a specific place. Clients with complex trauma may have had a few places where they felt calm, astonished, or surrounded by beauty. It is elegant to use these memories. However, imagine this scenario. I am introducing the calm scene exercise to the client and the client immediately says, "Maui… it has to be Maui… I can imagine it and go there in the snap of a finger." In this case, it's easy to use Maui, except that the client is coming to see me for divorce trauma and Maui was where they honeymooned. The client may not actually make the connection that the calm scene intersects the trauma we are working on until they are in the middle of it. Again, the calm scene shouldn't intersect with the reason they are coming to therapy.

Container Exercise

"I Don't Connect With It Strongly"

Sometimes, consultees will report that the client developed the container but didn't really have a strong positive emotional response to it. My reply is usually that "the container is a box that holds stuff… it's unusual for people to have a deep somatic experience with a box." The point of the exercise is to develop it as a mental construct and to send the message that the things we are containing are things we are putting up for right now.

"I Already Do This"

When I describe the container to a client, they sometimes have a strong emotional response. They say, "Tom, I already do this. In fact, I'm coming to you to help me stop doing this and here you are showing me to do something that I'm coming to you to show me how to stop." We need to patiently listen to the client and then explain that containment is actually a great gift of the nervous system since having trauma mostly out of awareness allows us to function when we need to. Containment for the purpose of avoiding can leave us stuck. However, with everything that we put into the container, we do so with a purposeful intention to return to it and fully process it. Containment allows us to work somewhere. For us to work successfully somewhere, everything else needs to be out of working memory. Practicing containment is a key skill that clients with complex trauma will need in order to do trauma work. With clients with complex trauma, not everything that knocks on the door of awareness should be encouraged to enter.

"I Shouldn't Have to Do This"

Clients may have an emotional response to the container exercise when they realize that they need to develop one. Clients may say, "It's unfair that I have to develop the container to hold what was done to me! I shouldn't have to do this." It is usually helpful to simply normalize that difficult reality.

I will sometimes say, "Yes, it is deeply unfair that we have to be both the prisoner and the jailer for what was done to us. The world should not have been set up that way, and I'm sorry that it is. I wish that things stuck to the person who did bad things rather than the person who they were done to... but that's not how things are."

"Can't I Just Burn It, Bury It, or Put It on a Rocket Ship?"

No. The purpose of the container is to hold things that we are not prepared to work on in this moment. With trauma, nothing buried I ever lost. If you want to use a rocket ship, we need to design it with a "Return Home" button so that it can return to us what we put into it when we are ready to deal with it.

"I'm Trying to Contain Everything and It Won't Go"

One of the most common problems with the container is when clients try to put trauma that is not currently in working memory into the container. The container is for things that are in right-now working memory that we are not prepared to work on in this moment. Sometimes clients will reach into their trauma container of the "limbic brain" memory storage and grab real trauma or whole themes of trauma and put it into the container. In order to contain something, we have to touch it. If we touch it, we bring it into working memory. In short, it is best practice to tell clients not to contain things that are not in right-now in working memory.

Light Stream

Other than problems visualizing discussed at the beginning of this chapter, most problems with light stream reduce to meanings associated with the "bright and healing light." For some people, the light has spiritual suggestions, and embodied shame may conflict or cause uncomfortable resonance when the light comes into contact with the internalized shame. Other people have medical trauma and the bright light is suggestive of emergency operating rooms.

For the first seven years that I was an EMDR therapist, I struggled with light stream for two reasons. One was spiritual trauma. I simply didn't want something suggestive of spirituality that close to me. The other was that I viewed my skin as a border with the outside world. My skin separates me from not me. If light is inside me, something has gone wrong with my border with the outside world. Imagining the bright healing light as sunshine and allowing the heat of the sun to warm my skin was my workable accommodation for light stream. You may need to help clients find their own accommodation or use other resources.

Chapter 28
The Utility of Containment

Container resources expedite the process of returning difficult content to the "limbic brain." Containers very often are a cognitive strategy or intention not to engage with something right now. A container can also include somatic sensations, because if we only address the cognitive aspects of rumination, we may be leaving a lot of distress in the body, which can reactivate the mind. Containers are also a helpful ritual in pivoting away from activation. It's a ritual that signifies something to parts. However, the reasons that we need to container matter.

Many problems with containment come from the assumptions that clients make about what containment means. For instance, what it means to current functioning, what it means for their past, and what it means for their recovery. For example, many clients may argue against containment as a form of avoidance.

Again, we need to explain clearly the intention of containment. All of these are good/healthy/adaptive reasons for containing something that has been activated:

- We have been trying to solve the problem using strategies that have a very long history of being ineffective (rumination, allowing lots of memories/cognitions/themes to connect).
- Now is not a good time to try to resolve the problem or issue.
- The issue is intruding on our ability to function at the present time.
- The problem is actively contributing to the current instability.
- We would like to exercise control over what is getting our attention in the current moment.
- Adaptive containment is ultimately about client agency… deciding on purpose what to attend to in this moment and what to defer, because we are not wired to attend to everything past/present/future in every moment.
- Containment is the beginning of stability.

Ultimately, we want to emphasize that it's okay to container because we have a plan to resolve this issue in an effective way at a later date using a transformational psychotherapy.

The following containers are not ideal:

- Diaper Genie
- Rocket
- Incinerator
- Trash can
- Explosive

Containment is one of the best adaptations of human evolution. The "limbic brain" is a container. We are information processing systems. When we encounter information that we cannot assimilate because we were too shut down, too overwhelmed, or lacked the needed adaptive information at the time, it is helpful to have a place to put it until we can try again to assimilate it.

Clients often come to us with a lot of ambivalence about carrying a lot of contained experiences. On one hand, they have been consciously and unconsciously trying to process (or at least manage) this information using incredibly ineffective strategies for all of their lives. On the other, they have visceral experiences (all of them bad) from trying to purposefully interact with contained information. Containing isn't a neutral activity. Asking a client to simply let go of information that is both existentially salient and intractable is not a neutral ask. Everything we container, past interactions with the container, past strategies to try to process trauma, and the fact that we are carrying stuff that needs containment are all implicated in what makes purposeful containment difficult for many clients with complex trauma.

Containment Isn't Just for the Visual Stuff

The way we often teach containment is as a visualization resource. It is helpful to know if your clients struggle with visualization, and many will. Again, containment is a metaphor and also a ritual. A lot of people don't intuitively understand metaphors. A lot of people don't resonate with rituals, particularly visual rituals. If we appreciate how hard the minds of our clients are working to keep them safe every minute, difficulties with visualization make sense. For a practical example of this, imagine slowly counting from 10 down to zero. As you are doing that, subtract that number from 10. So, 10-10 = 0; 10-9 =1; etc. While you are doing this, try to imagine the calm scene of a beach, the waves, seagulls, sand, sky, sun, clouds, and sounds. Now, try doing all of this with your eyes open, because closing your eyes may make anxiety or disconnection from the present more noticeable.

Imagining something like a container is a creative task, and the creative parts of the brain aren't strongly online when our nervous system thinks we're at war. Again, very few works of great literature were written in the trenches of Europe.

Sometimes, the problem with visualization isn't related to the container itself but to identifying what to container and trying to find a "handle" on the material. One of the things we might contain is our body-based sensations from the activation. The ShopVac resource from the Four Blinks Version of Flash is a helpful resource for containing body-based activation quickly.

Test the Container With Something Other Than Trauma

When working with clients with complex trauma, one of the common mistakes I see in many scripts is asking people to test the container using pieces of actual trauma when developing the container. I like to test the container using something innocuous, like a business card or a slip of paper. Testing the container using something neutral is something that is built into the Four Blinks Version of Flash script and can give us some confidence that containment works without substantial risk of overactivation.

Sensory Grounding (And Other Resources) Are Also Containment Strategies

If we think about what is broadly happening with containment, there are many ways that we may be able to do it other than using the standard Shapiro container resource. Sensory grounding is also a containment strategy in the sense that a lot of rumination and trauma activation happens in an abstracted (perhaps even partially dissociated) state. Finding our way into the "safety" of the present can help create the conditions that can quickly allow material in awareness to find its way back into the trauma containers of the limbic brain. Sensory grounding can help us briefly escape processes that may be feeding activation. Sensory grounding is also a great way to transition to containment and to help make sure that we have enough footing in the present and increase the chances that containment will work effectively... at least for a while.

What Does It Mean When Clients Say That Containment Doesn't Work for Them?

Want to be respectful when a client says that something doesn't work, but there is also information in it. That information is essential so that we can help navigate these difficulties. Sometimes, a client's problem containing reduces to one of the following:

- I have to keep doing it. It doesn't stay contained.
- Parts of me don't want to put this issue away for now.
- It's probably not one thing that needs to be contained. When content seeps into awareness and rumination starts, clients with complex trauma often do not have one thing to container. They will often struggle to find a handle or a perspective on the material once they have been handling it for a while. It's easier to contain fragments of memory for many people than it is to contain whole themes, particularly when those themes connect to core needs, so we should show clients how to container a piece of it.

Chapter 29
"And Then the Client Dissociated"

In 2024, look around almost any room in almost any context, and many (if not most) people are dissociated into their smartphones. This is true in coffee shops when couples are sitting across from each other. This is true in the lines of amusement parks, under umbrellas on beaches, whether alone or not in living rooms, and in many classrooms. People in the United States currently spend about 60 hours a week actively engaged with their phones or related screens, with no indication of slow-down. This is more time than most of us will spend sleeping, actively working, doing our hobbies, engaging in our other addictions, or actively interacting with family. Zoom out and we resemble a pervasively dissociated culture. Zoom out more and even a sensible person might wonder if it is paranoid to question if the whole point of Western Civilization is to pervasively distract ourselves from ourselves.

Dissociation is a completely normal part of human experience. Dissociation, even in the most extreme forms, is a completely normal part of human experience when it intersects with extreme awfulness. This obsession among trauma therapists with the "problem" of dissociation is highly troubling. It gets blamed for everything. It is a symptom of problems. It is also a reasonable and understandable survival response. My own dissociative impulses were some of the most creative and sensible adaptations that I made as a child and young adult. My dissociation allowed me to do amazing things in the world as a teen and a young adult. Yes, these processes had costs. Trauma is the problem. Trauma is why we can't have nice things. It's why we needed, and continue to need, to dissociate. We need to find ways to stop blaming the symptoms of trauma for our difficulty in treating trauma.

Before we can explore ways to work more effectively in EMDR therapy with clients whose system has survived using dissociative processes, we need to clarify some of the ways that dissociation might show up and how each might be problematic to the tasks of EMDR therapy, or not. For instance, when a consultee reviewing a case says, "and then the client dissociated," I never quite know what he means. When I inquire more, sometimes they describe an emotional or somatic shutdown response. I might explore more, and we intuit that the client is stuck in the huge existential loneliness of childhood, which looks and feels dissociative. Sometimes they describe a flashback experience. Other times they say that the client started "ugly crying," "lost the target memory," engaged in avoidant strategies, or switched to a different ego state. These are remarkably different processes that all fall under the term "dissociation." Dissociation, it seems, is like a black box that we throw all of the things loosely associated with the freeze response into. As a linguistic term and a cultural artifact, it is weirdly and suspiciously imprecise. We have dozens of words to describe varieties of coffee and many dozens of words to describe the varieties and subvarieties of wine, but only one word that we consistently use to describe all of these different "problematic" processes in EMDR therapy.

What Are We Asking Clients to Do in EMDR Therapy?

As stated in the Tricycle metaphor and elsewhere, we can boil the tasks of EMDR therapy down to three central components: activate (but do not overactivate) a part of a memory, notice the results of that activation deeply in the present, and do this while your nervous system is receiving a left-right stimulation. Different types of dissociation might make it difficult for clients to engage in the activation and noticing components of EMDR therapy. I'll attempt to account for the most common ways that clients who have survived by utilizing dissociative responses encounter difficulties in EMDR therapy through the lenses of the tasks of activation and noticing.

Overactivation and Underactivation

Activation is a core part of the EMDR therapy process. Clients need to tolerably activate a piece of a tolerable memory. There are many reasons clients may struggle with either overactivation or underactivation.

Many people have a system of parts. Many of those parts are organized to keep the system safe and to protect the system from accessing trauma in unadvisable ways. Parts know how to do their roles well. I also recognize that the client's parts have a view of the client's internal world that I do not have. I am respectful of their perspective. I express interest in helping the client understand their parts system more fully and promote ways that the client's system can communicate internally more effectively.

I express interest in allowing their parts system to get to know me. EMDR is a collaborative process with the client's parts. I ask for consent to engage in resources. I ask if it is a good idea from the perspective of all parts to work on a particular memory on any given day.

When parts are not consulted from a place of openness, they may prevent activation as a defensive strategy. My tendency is to assume that they know more than I do. I inquire if there is a territory that feels safer to work in today and we try to work there. When parts are not consulted or the body starts to feel a way that feels intolerable (or parts think things may move in that direction), overactivation as a defensive or distraction strategy can occur. Asking for client consent in all phases of EMDR therapy is an excellent modification when working with a client's parts system.

Somatic Dissociation

Do not assume that your clients with complex trauma are embodied enough to notice. They may live in a pervasively dissociated somatic state or may "snap" into a somatically dissociated state when overactivated. When clients aren't in their bodies enough to notice, activation is challenging because emotions may be little more than thoughts about feelings. Somatic dissociation is a survival strategy that helped many of us survive previously intolerable somatic states. And yes, once parts of us learn how to go away and disconnect from our bodies, it's easy to snap there even when we are able to be somatically present during other less stressful parts of our lives. When clients are pervasively shut down in their bodies, EMDR therapy will be a goose chase until they are able to be embodied enough to notice. When somatic shutdown responses come as a result of activation, it often comes as a symptom of overactivation. Overactivation is something that we can try to manage using other strategies. Later chapters describe how to help clients stay more somatically present with distress by changing how the client interacts with the memory in order to help promote distress coming into awareness at more tolerable rates and intensities.

Disconnection from the Present

All noticing that is productive in EMDR therapy happens in the present moment and through the body of the client's right-now nervous system. Many new therapists complain about the "problem" of dissociation when clients seem to disconnect from their current experience and seem to not be present in the room during some parts of reprocessing. When clients seem to disconnect from the present, where do they usually go? The vast majority of the time when the client "leaves the room" they are simply interacting with the bad memory too deeply. It is a problem that is quickly resolved with well-practiced grounding resources. Disconnection from the present moment can be problematic in EMDR therapy because all noticing that produces healing happens in the present moment. If the client keeps dissociating into the memory, we need to strengthen grounding skills, remind the client to anchor awareness in the present, and bring as much "stuff" (smells, objects, hot or cold drinks, weighted blankets, stuffed animals, etc.) into session as we can to help the client stay grounded. If enhanced grounding strategies and changing how the client is interacting with the memory isn't helpful enough, I highly recommend working in a different memory territory that is more tolerable. Tolerable means, among other things, that the client can be present and notice it in the right-now body.

Heavy rumination, or trying to figure out the trauma, often looks a lot like dissociation from the present moment. Check with the client and get their GPS coordinates in the check-in. If they appear stuck in cognitive or ruminative processes, introduce a perspective change or a channel change (ideally toward the body or toward noticing in this present moment).

If the client is not dissociating into the bad memory or into ruminative processes but simply appears to be disconnected from the present moment, it is probable that the disconnection is happening as a symptom of overactivation. Dissociation inside EMDR therapy is often a symptom of overactivation. In these cases, overactivation is the problem. Dissociating from overactivation is not the problem. Dissociation is not evidence that the client cannot do EMDR therapy. It is not evidence that we need to endlessly return to Phase Two to resolve the "problem of dissociation." If the client is disconnecting from present experience because of overactivation, then the client's dissociative response was one of the best things that was going to happen in that session. We need to find ways to modulate the activation. We need to work in memory territories with clients with complex trauma that are at the intersection of productive and tolerable and we need to help the client interact with pieces of the memory content in ways that are tolerable enough for them to be able to notice and digest in the present moment.

Chapter 30
Blocking Beliefs are Also Phase Two Problems

It is helpful to think of a blocking belief as any negative belief about the self that impairs the client's ability to do one of the core tasks of EMDR therapy. "It's not safe to feel my emotions" isn't a blocking belief because it has limited the client's ability to function in healthy ways. It's a block in EMDR therapy because the core tasks of EMDR therapy require that the client activate a difficult memory and notice that activation. Activation and noticing are unlikely to be successful in a client who does not feel safe enough to activate, experience, and notice emotions. If the client has this block, we need to work with the client to help the client feel safe enough to experience and notice enough activation for EMDR therapy to be productive.

Blocking beliefs are not blocks in EMDR therapy because the child parts of the client believe them. They are blocks because the client's right-now parts also believe them. Blocking beliefs are often survival strategies that were utilized across many developmental eras, including the present.

Typical guidance by trainers and consultants is to target the memories that originally created the blocking belief, but with clients with complex trauma, this may also be much bigger memory territory than is advisable for the initial targets. The block may take offline much of what is needed to resolve the memories that initially caused it. We may need to challenge the block in other ways prior to starting the processing phases of EMDR therapy. Some strategies to do this include psychoeducation, perspective-taking exercises, parts work, and exploration of these blocks as survival strategies. I prefer to start chipping away at blocking beliefs in Phase Two, assuming I am aware of them in the preparation phases of EMDR therapy.

The following are some of the most common blocking beliefs and how they manifest as blocks in EMDR therapy:

- "I can't show my emotions" often shows up as problems activating and noticing.

- "I have to be perfect" often results in clients focusing on their performance in therapy rather than noticing activation from the target memory.
- "I can't handle it" may prevent activation or cause the client to shut down when attempting to notice difficult somatic states.
- "I am bad/don't deserve to heal" functions as an answer to "why" the trauma happened, yet traumatic information cannot connect to it because you cannot connect a lie to a lie in EMDR therapy.

I use many of the strategies below to help clients scrutinize these beliefs in ways that may also help them develop the needed adaptive information. When possible, these interventions are best done outside of the EMDR reprocessing phases.

Psychoeducation

Blocking beliefs typically reflect deficits in adaptive information. What makes them "blocking" is that the deficit impairs one of the central tasks needed to perform EMDR therapy well. Attachment wounding is wounding in multiple ways. It is wounding to be born with hard-wired needs that are not met. It is additionally wounding to have missed out on the adaptive information that comes from the experience of getting needs met. To make matters worse, not getting needs met typically requires coping or survival strategies to manage the unmet needs and these strategies often compound the developmental disruptions (i.e., numbing, dissociation, addictions, or problematic enactments). As learning experiences, attachment wounds are repeatedly and redundantly experienced and encoded. They make up the fabric of what is normal and expected. The information contained in this learning is salient, and the lessons are often essential for surviving childhood. Ultimately, these developmental deficits typically compound and confuse the client's nervous system by inserting false information in the place where adaptive information should have been stored.

It's easy to believe what was modeled, positive or negative. When children are born to people who do not have the capacity to meet their needs consistently, those people often blame the children for having those needs. Children are easily confused about their needs and whose responsibility it is to meet them. When children grow into adults and have not had enough corrective experiences of getting their needs met in healthy ways, they may remain confused. Many trauma therapists have experienced the challenges of trying to explain the realities of childhood needs to severely traumatized clients in ways that resonate with their experience. Often my initial task is to carefully provide accurate information about what it means to be born human. This initial psychoeducation is the seed. Over subsequent sessions, I'll use some of the strategies below in the hope of constructing initial and tentative experiential instances of adaptive learning that we can supplement and grow.

Psychoeducation typically touches on the following categories of adaptive information, depending on the client's needs and informational deficits:

- Children are born with needs and cannot meet their own needs.
- Children are not responsible for what grown-ups do to them.
- Children who struggle to get their needs met are placed in an impossible position. There are no good or ideal options. The options typically have advantages and costs.
- Children's needs are broad, comprehensive, and nonnegotiable.
- Meeting the emotional needs of grown-ups is developmentally disruptive for a child.
- Not getting needs met when young may create deficits that are developmental, neurobiological, social, and psychological.
- We learn experientially and develop pathways of healing experientially. Some of these pathways that we may need to create may allow for easier and more effective communication between different parts of you and across different developmental eras.

I anticipate that very little of this "information" will strongly resonate with most clients. Clients will also need to have experiences that might help make this information actionable to the nervous system. Experiences are the enzymes that can help turn psychoeducation into tentative, usable, and adaptive information.

Perspective-Taking Exercises to Challenge Blocking Beliefs

One of the strategies that can be helpful to experientially disconfirm blocks is through perspective-taking exercises. I may invite the client outside of EMDR reprocessing to imagine a friend or someone else in a similar situation and ask the client what advice they would give that person. This may allow opportunities to explore the presence of adaptive information and why the client believes the adaptive information that applies to others does not apply to himself.

Another helpful perspective-taking exercise is to explore instances in the client's life when they are already living in ways that violate the blocking belief. For instance, if the client has a blocking belief related to "I can't show my emotions," I may explore the times with this belief may not have been true. The client may report a close relationship with a pet; I may explore a time when the pet did something funny, and the client caught himself laughing. Highlighting important ways that the client may already be violating the rules built into the block can be a helpful way to scrutinize the block. Encouraging the client to experientially reconnect with the memories that disconfirm the block can be helpful. "When you bring up that memory now, what are you noticing?" Even as we are getting in touch with small moments of exceptions, it is important not to minimize the many other contexts where the block may hold and may be experienced as true.

In the event of a block related to "I'm bad" or "I don't deserve to heal/get my needs met," I may explore if the client believes that block across all parts of the self. I will invite the client to get in touch with the most adult or wise parts to see if that part believes that he has always been this way. If the client reports that the negative belief feels like it has always been true, I will invite the client to go on a journey in imagination with me:

> Can you imagine me and you magically traveling to a large hospital nursery with newborn babies coming and going? Can you imagine them in their little carts? Which of those babies deserve to have their needs met today? Can we sort out which ones of them are bad?

I explain to the client that in 1970, I was one of those babies. I explain that in the year he was born, he was one of those babies. This thought experiment opens the door to explore the possibility that this belief emerged as a survival strategy, rather than an objective and dispositional state of reality at birth.

Exploring Blocking Beliefs as a Survival Strategy

In cases where the blocking belief is, "It's not safe to experience my emotions," I am likely to remind the client that he was not born that way. I may ask the client what he thinks he was doing immediately after he was born. The client will often report that he was probably crying. I may explain:

> When I hear you say that, it makes me believe that you were born with the capacity to express your emotions and needs with your whole voice and your whole body… I wonder if the belief that you can't experience your emotions is one that came later. If it came later, then that may mean that this isn't how you *are* but rather is what you had to learn how to be in order to get your needs met or avoid trouble.

Once the client is able to identify that a blocking belief is a survival strategy that was developed for survival, we can begin the process of exploring how it developed, why it developed, the life circumstances that enhanced and shaped its development, and how it is still maintained. In short, we can explore how this block helped you survive. What has it cost you to have survived in that way? Exploring the costs of blocking beliefs can be a helpful strategy to assess motivation to change, particularly if the blocking belief appears to have long outlived its utility as a safety strategy in the client's current life.

Parts Work Interventions

One of the most elegant ways to scrutinize blocking beliefs is through the process of parts work. Again in my conceptualization, a well-developed and well-practiced attachment figure resource is one way to do parts work in an expedited fashion. In other therapies, we might send the client out into the world to have disconfirming experiences with others that challenge the blocking belief. Sending a client with a pervasively traumatized nervous system out to have disconfirming experiences is likely to result in additional confirmation of the expectations in the bad memories since these clients are likely to date and conduct friendships in ways consistent with their sense of value and self-worth. Parts work is a way for parts of us to have disconfirming relational experiences with other parts of ourselves. An attachment figure resource is not a "part," but it brings nurture and adaptive information to parts who have experienced deficits in getting needs met and does so within view of many of the other present client parts. When a part of the client feels unlovable and undeserving of attention, the attachment figure resource can bring in an imaginal way what was developmentally missing. When clients have experiences receiving nurture and adaptive information, it is harder for their parts to believe that they are undeserving of it. Parts work in its various forms can help clients scrutinize blocks and have experiences that allow the psychoeducation components to be made more actionable in the client's nervous system.

Interventions From Other Psychotherapies

It is often an asset when clients come to EMDR therapy having previously engaged in Cognitive-Behavioral Therapy (CBT), Cognitive Processing Therapy (CPT), or Dialectical Behavioral Therapy (DBT). These therapies, when conducted sensitively and well, can help clients develop the needed adaptive information and effectively scrutinize blocking beliefs. They can help the client frontload the needed adaptive information.

How to Know When a Block is Adequately Resolved?

Blocking beliefs are a problem in EMDR therapy because they take up space where adaptive information should be stored, and they do this in the parts of the self where the trauma will need to be metabolized into (typically the resourced parts). Again, a block is a block in EMDR therapy because it is shared between parts. A block emerges when your child parts and your most resourced adult parts believe, for instance, that it is not safe to experience your emotions. From the standpoint of the boat metaphor, a blocking belief functions like large boxes in the client's canoe of adaptive information. Because they take up needed space, they block the capacity to land fish of any real size into the canoe.

You will know that a block has been resolved enough for EMDR therapy to potentially be effective in the territory of the block when the client can identify a discrepancy between what they know is true versus how it feels when they think about a particular memory. For instance, the client may say the following: "I know that children are not responsible for what grown-ups do to them, but when I think about that memory from when I was six years old, I just feel so guilty."

Or they may say: "Parts of me know that I should have been taken care of, but when I think of my childhood it feels like people abandoned me because I was a bad child." A VOC of one might be a canary in the coal mine here and essentially means that no part of the client believes that the positive cognition might be true. In EMDR therapy, discrepancies between what we know and what we feel are a strong indicator of the presence of adaptive information and also stuck information. When all parts of the self believe only the negative lesson in the trauma, that is a strong indicator that the client does not have an adequate enough fund of adaptive information for EMDR therapy to be successful around that type of target at this time. Additional resourcing or working in adjacent memory territories may be needed to help build the needed adaptive information.

Chapter 31
What Does Prepared Enough Mean?

A common consultation question is, "How do I know when a particular client is prepared enough to start the processing phases of EMDR therapy?"

My response is often, "Prepared enough to start where?" Very few clients with extreme trauma will be prepared enough to start with the earliest or worst traumatic experiences first, even with extensive preparation. We may need to work on smaller memories first in order to help build enough of the adaptive information needed to tackle the heftiest ones later in treatment. From the perspective of the boat metaphor, catching smaller fish first allows clients to develop what will be needed to handle the larger ones effectively. Also, catching smaller fish generates the assets we need to have a bigger boat.

How Do We Know When Clients Are Prepared to Start Somewhere?

It is difficult to know for sure when clients are prepared enough to start the EMDR therapy reprocessing phases. It is important to allow people to start reprocessing if they are equipped for the journey. However, we don't want the preparation phases to be like a height line necessary to ride a ride at the county fair. It's easy to endlessly declare clients with complex trauma "not ready" for the reprocessing phases. Our job is to help the client develop what is needed for them to be prepared for the tasks of EMDR therapy. The following sections itemize the minimum requirements that I consider when deciding if the client is prepared to start reprocessing somewhere.

The Client Understands EMDR Therapy Well Enough to Give Consent

EMDR therapy often requires that clients sit for long periods with substantial distress. Most clients process this distress somatically by slowing down, being present with it, and noticing it deeply. This is a difficult task for people who may have survived their trauma by staying ahead of it, not slowing down, avoiding, and not noticing. Clients who do EMDR therapy well understand fully what they are getting into, and they understand how to, and are prepared to do their job in this dance well. It is helpful to walk clients with complex trauma through the protocol, so that they understand the elements of this approach. Clients may come to therapy seeking EMDR, but it is important to try to understand what they think EMDR therapy is, how it is conducted, and their sense of what is required of them. EMDR therapy for complex trauma needs to be built around the understanding that recovering from complex trauma will not happen quickly, effortlessly, and without any risk.

Does the client understand that EMDR therapy involves activating a piece of a difficult experience, slowing down, and noticing deeply the right-now impact of that activation on the nervous system? Preparing the client to do EMDR therapy prepares them to do the core tasks required by this therapy. Does the client understand that doing almost anything other than what I am asking her to do is very likely to cause problems inside reprocessing? The client should understand what EMDR therapy is and should clearly understand that EMDR therapy is not any of the following:

- A think-think session where the client ruminates about the memory the same way they do outside of an EMDR therapy session.
- An opportunity to try to resolve the whole theme or other clusters of memory connected to the memory we are targeting.
- A chance to purposefully put the right thoughts in the correct order.
- A way to make sense of existential questions.
- A way to resolve a lifetime of trauma quickly and without distress.

The Client Needs to Feel Safe Enough in the Present

EMDR therapy requires that clients have the capacity to activate a piece of memory, slow down, feel safe enough in the present moment to notice the distress that emerges and do these tasks for extended periods at a time. It is essential that therapists realize that a lot of what we are asking the client to do in Phase Two tests the client's capacity to slow down, feel safe enough in the present moment, and notice deeply current experience. For this reason, problems in Phase Two are strong warning signs for the reprocessing phases. If the therapist misses that the client is struggling to slow down, connect with a sense of safety in the present, and stay grounded, the therapist may move the client into reprocessing phases and will encounter predictable and unfortunate results. If the client cannot slow down and connect with the present moment, that client is not prepared to do EMDR therapy currently. If the client cannot tolerably activate even a small difficult experience, that client is not prepared to do EMDR therapy at this moment. If simply noticing that he is in a human body that is breathing causes panic symptoms, that client is not ready for EMDR therapy today. We need to help the client develop the capacity to do the tasks that we are asking her to do in the reprocessing phases. If the client cannot do one of the core tasks, they are not prepared to engage in EMDR therapy. No task of EMDR therapy is more central than present-based noticing.

The Client Needs to Be Able to Regulate Activation on Purpose

Trauma and trauma activation often push the client's gas pedal. Overactivation causes many difficulties in EMDR therapy, including pushing the needed adaptive information farther away. In order to do trauma work safely, clients need to have regulation strategies in place, and these resources need to reliably work when needed. Resources are the brake pedal. I will sometimes tell clients that EMDR therapy is a journey, but it wouldn't be wise for me to go across the street with them in a car that does not have a brake. I am not picky about which regulation strategies "work" for the client if these resources can be done in session reliably and effectively. Also, I anticipate that most mindfulness strategies will not make an 8/10 level of distress a 1/10 level of distress. It does not need to, nor would that feel safe with most clients with complex trauma. If a resource decreases activation some, then it is a good resource to use. I consider a resource rugged enough to use in sessions with clients with complex trauma if the resource has worked in session and the client can identify times outside of session when the resource was helpful in regulating distress. Many difficult things happen when the client overactivates in an EMDR session. Without adequate regulation strategies, these difficulties may directly impair the client's ability to do EMDR therapy well, effectively, and safely.

Is the Client Embodied Enough to Notice?

EMDR therapy is a bottom-up psychotherapy. Is the client embodied enough to notice? If not, EMDR therapy is likely to be a goose chase. Often a quick Dip Your Toe In Body Scan can reveal how aware the client is of baseline distress. If they are not embodied enough to notice, we engage in exercises to help bring online body awareness. A client who is not embodied enough to notice may report no distress in parts of the body below the jaw despite complaints of frequent anxiety and panic symptoms. Emotions without body activation are often just thoughts about feelings.

Does the Client Have the Capacity to Feel Worse Today?

EMDR therapy typically is a dive into distress. Clients need to have at least some capacity to feel worse today in order to engage in EMDR therapy effectively. Some clients will come to sessions without the energy needed to do reprocessing. For clients who come to the session on the edge of panic or who appear the most depressed I have ever seen them, therapy will likely involve interventions other than EMDR reprocessing to help them become more stable and less acutely distressed.

Does the Client Have Enough Adaptive Information for the Current Memory Territory?

At its core EMDR therapy involves connecting old stuck information into right-now existing adaptive information. EMDR therapy does not create additional adaptive information simply because it is needed. Using the boat metaphor, the client will not get a bigger boat simply because he is connected to a large shark. He has the boat that he launched with today. The client must have enough of the needed adaptive information for the difficult information to link up to. It is important to understand that adaptive information is not one thing. The client may have adequate information in one domain but may have profound deficits in others. Again, it is helpful to work where there are discrepancies between what the client knows is true and how the memory feels in the present moment, i.e. "I know that kids are not responsible for what adults do to them, but when I think about that memory, I just feel so guilty."

Phases Three-Seven

"During EMDR, I was able to conjure two separate, simultaneous versions of myself – the child version and the present version. I was able to feel child Stephanie's emotions and my own. I was able to comfort her with my present wisdom. I was able to simultaneously be the one giving love and the one receiving it."

--Stephanie Foo, *What My Bones Know*

Chapter 32
The Utility of Informed Consent

It is possible for clients to be harmed by EMDR therapy if they do not expect that difficulties may appear and do not have a clear plan and resources in place to manage those difficulties. Challenges in EMDR therapy are not limited to the processing phases. Difficulties can emerge and cause trauma responses in Phase One and Two.

Clients with complex trauma will need to be able to consent to the work that they do, and we will need to provide clear information about each step. Their parts will need to consent to the work that we are asking them to do. It is important to explore the risks of doing this work and also the risks of not doing this work. Often the risks of not healing are substantial and life-long. Part of what is unique about our professions is that we see and understand the past, present, and future risks and consequences of not healing from complex trauma.

Asking for consent at every phase of EMDR therapy allows the client's parts to collaborate and for client concerns related to a resource or a target to appear prior to engagement with it. Clients may be more willing to engage in difficult work if they know that their therapist values consent and that the therapist is able to effectively manage the concerns and agendas of parts of themselves. In order to give consent, clients need to understand what we will ask them to do and why.

For resources, it can be helpful to describe the resource to the client before engaging in it. This allows the client to describe their concerns about this resource. If the client communicates that exercises like this do not work for him, we can explore how we might be able to do the resource differently enough from previous times for it to be worth the experiment.

For the processing phases, it is helpful to walk the client through the Phase Three-Seven script so that we are able to explain what we will be asking them to do and why. EMDR therapy is a dance, and a client that is well educated about what is coming and how to do those tasks may allow them to do them well. A client that is well informed about their role in the dance may make it less likely that they will also try to do my role as therapist in the dance.

As we are working with the client to select the memory at the beginning of Phase Three, the following quick question is very helpful: *"**Do all parts of you think working on this memory today is a good idea?**"* If so, continue. If not, see if any part has a resolvable concern, and then work with the parts to find a memory that feels safer or more tolerable for today.

A lot of wounding with clients with complex trauma has occurred in contexts absent consent. Consent is a core modern human value that is good to model in all contexts between two adult humans. Opening the door to consent opens the door to essential conversations and explorations that can make everything we are trying to accomplish easier and more equitable.

Being open to client consent means that sometimes therapy does not go exactly the way the therapist imagined. When consent feels like a tax, inefficiency, or burden for the therapist, the therapist should check for the presence of agenda, privilege, or power.

Chapter 33
Helping Clients Understand Their Role in This Dance

Absent clear guidance about how to "do" EMDR therapy, clients will generally try to resolve the memory in the reprocessing phases using the same strategies that they do outside of EMDR therapy when their bodies feel similar ways. They will try to solve the trauma using ways that are intuitive, familiar, and ineffective. We engage in EMDR therapy because it is different from the approaches that clients have spent their lives practicing. EMDR sessions are not a power think-think session. If we approach healing in EMDR therapy too abruptly or with too much agenda, healing will run from us. When healing comes, it comes to us slowly and as a byproduct of deep present-based noticing. There is nothing to figure out. The right thoughts come to us as a function of healing. We don't create them with intention or use our neocortex to purposefully assemble the right thoughts in just the right order.

Before educating clients with complex trauma about how to do their role in EMDR therapy well, I'd like to begin with several strong suggestions for therapists that are different from standard orientation guidance. It is common for therapists to instruct new EMDR therapy clients to "let things go where they go" and have "one foot in the past, one foot in the present." This is rarely the best guidance for clients with complex trauma when they are at the very beginning of their EMDR journey. As we are able to verify that clients are able to do the core tasks that we are asking them to do, we can start to experiment with removing any of the initial restrictions that we put in place. Starting reprocessing with fully unrestricted processing that promotes anything and everything coming into awareness is a recipe for overactivation with most clients with complex trauma.

Don't "Let Things Go Where They Go"

With relatively healthy clients with wide windows of tolerance, it is important that we not construct obstacles that interfere with the client's noticing. In short, we want to let the client's awareness go wherever it needs to go in the service of healing. Staying out of the way allows plenty of space for insight to appear. It allows the client to form essential connections between different categories and aspects of wounding.

Clients with complex trauma typically have very narrow windows of tolerance, enormous volumes of closely related and highly volatile traumatic content, and extremely limited adaptive information for the difficult information to be metabolized into. As highlighted elsewhere in this book, we need distressing content to come, but it needs to come at a digestible rate and intensity. Allowing too much distress to come into awareness too soon is an invitation for overactivation. My primary goal is to help the client start somewhere and take steps to increase the chances that the client has a productive experience trying to digest the memory we started with. Anticipate that with many clients with complex trauma "letting things go where they go" will want to go everywhere. If you allow things to go everywhere in reprocessing with many clients with complex trauma, you will get nowhere.

Don't "Have One Foot in the Past, One Foot in the Present"

Consistent with other sections of this book, we need memory content to come, but we need it to come at digestible rates and intensities. Clients with complex trauma are highly likely to overly-dissociate into the memory. This is a problem in EMDR therapy because all noticing that is productive must happen in the present moment and in the client's right-now nervous system. I am not encouraging clients with complex trauma to "have one foot in the past and one foot in the present." That is an invitation for the client to be half dissociated in the past. I want my clients with complex trauma to glance at the bad memory and "take a bite" of it. I want all the client's focus to be directed to noticing and digesting the last piece of activation. Metaphorically, leaving a barn door wide open leaves the client exposed to trampling horses, cows, pigs, or anything else that wants to rush out.

Yes, this is a slight restriction on reprocessing. Taking more digestible bites of the memory with clients with complex trauma is often the only effective way to work. Do not use restrictions like this with healthier or more resourced clients. Remove these restrictions when they are no longer needed for safe and effective reprocessing.

The Brownie Mix of EMDR Therapy

Similar to the Tricycle metaphor, the Brownie Mix metaphor assumes that doing EMDR therapy as the client involves several very simple ingredients. If clients are not clear about what the elements of EMDR are, what noticing means and how to do it, how to interact with the memory, and how to avoid strong agendas, it is easy to mix into EMDR therapy ingredients (like corn or green beans) that may mess up the brownie mix. It is helpful to clarify the client's role and the therapist's role in this therapy, or the client may attempt to do both.

I describe EMDR therapy reprocessing as consisting of three core ingredients: activate a specific memory (but do not overactive), notice deeply what comes up as a result of that activation, and do these things while your nervous system is experiencing a bilateral stimulation. This is the core of the brownie mix. During the vast majority of the session, I expect that the client will be engaged in deep present-based noticing and digesting the distress that they were too overwhelmed, too shut down, or didn't have the accessible adaptive information needed to metabolize at the time that the memory happened. If the client is doing anything else, they may be stirring creamed corn into the brownie mix of EMDR therapy. These stray ingredients may include trying to figure out the trauma, actively pulling in too much memory content, trying to evaluate their performance as the client, noticing unproductive channels, or noticing the distress in the memory but not doing so in the present moment/present body.

Be Concrete About What Noticing Means

It is entirely possible that many of your clients will not know what "notice that" means. Noticing is an active verb in EMDR therapy, and it is not a culturally intuitive activity in many of the cultures that wound people with complex trauma. Noticing is different from simple awareness. I often use the following language to orient clients to what noticing means, particularly when noticing body sensations.

> If you have sensations in your body during EMDR therapy, it can be helpful to scan your body and find the place of most distress and just notice its qualities deeply. Does it have a color, shape, or texture? Can

you trace its boundary with your awareness? Is it heavy or light? Does it have the same density throughout? Is it moving or still? Does it have an impulse or want to do something? Notice it as if it were an object in the world. Notice its qualities deeply, starting with its shape. Notice it like you are about to sketch it or draw it.

Many clients may be aware that they are experiencing an emotion, for instance, but are not noticing how that experience is appearing in the body. EMDR therapy is a somatic psychotherapy. The reprocessing phases start and end with the body for a reason. Nearly all of the transformational EMDR sessions I have observed involved the client spending much of the first half of the session observing somatic distress. Teaching clients what noticing means is a Phase Two skill. You don't want to first discover that clients have no idea what noticing means the moment you move into Phase Four for the first time.

Walking Clients Through the Protocol

One of the most helpful ways to orient clients to EMDR therapy is to walk them through the Phase Three through Seven script. This allows you to give clear psychoeducation at each stage with common examples. It also allows clients to clearly understand what is expected of them in all of the processing phases. It creates the possibility for clients and client parts to give full and informed consent to this process.

When You Start, You Will Get More Information. Use It.

Starting somewhere tolerable with clients with complex trauma will generate needed information. If processing goes smoothly and the client is able to manage all aspects of reprocessing, that is very helpful information about this client's nervous system and their accessible fund of adaptive information for this type of memory. If clients struggle in EMDR therapy, that struggle is also communicating essential information needed so that adjustments can be made. EMDR therapy may be difficult, but it must be tolerable. It must not cause the client to decompensate. As with every other effective psychotherapy with clients with complex trauma, we strive to work at the intersection of what is productive and what is tolerable. There is nowhere else to work, nowhere else to start. Starting somewhere will help clarify where those borders are.

Chapter 34
There Is Nothing to Figure Out Today

In order to do EMDR therapy effectively, clients need to have enough of the needed adaptive information present somewhere in their system. EMDR therapy is the connection of stuck information to right-now existing adaptive information. However, this connection generally happens to the client as a function of slowing down, being present, and noticing deeply the distress that emerges. A lot of what clients typically notice in the first half (or more) of an EMDR therapy session is distress, and much of this distress is of the somatic type. It is highly likely that clients are trying to "make sense" of the trauma or are trying to bypass the somatic distress of it when adaptive thoughts strongly appear soon after they transition into Phase Four. I am generally skeptical of adaptive information when it shows up too quickly, too strongly, or when it does not appear as the shadow cast by a substantial amount of distress. EMDR therapy typically is a dive into distress. Some clients seem to pivot out of the dive the moment they break the surface of distress. This is important information to observe, and it may be necessary to inquire with the client about their comfort or capacity to simply notice the distress that appears instead of immediately trying to fix it or avoid it.

Clients inside EMDR therapy will typically default to the same processes and behaviors that they do when they get somatically activated outside of EMDR therapy. They will engage in these familiar behaviors despite clear guidance and instruction by the therapist to do otherwise. Clients whose default response to trauma is to try to figure it out or ruminate about it will do this in EMDR therapy. Clients who are accustomed to overactivating and then collapsing into a shutdown response will do the same in EMDR therapy. Clients whose core survival strategies are to avoid, not slow down, and not be present with distress are very likely to avoid, stay ahead of it, and disconnect from distress inside their EMDR therapy.

Again, our goal in doing EMDR therapy is to engage in processes that are different from the client's usual, intuitive, and ineffective strategies. As part of EMDR therapy orientation, it is helpful to explain something like the following (and you may need to repeatedly remind them of this):

> EMDR therapy is different from our usual approaches to trying to make sense of trauma. There is nothing to figure out today. I'll remind the parts of you that want to make logical, rational, and reasonable sense of your experiences that most forms of trauma are inherently nonsensical. Also, you have spent decades thinking about your traumas, and there is nothing about thinking about them with bilateral stimulation that will allow you to purposefully make sense of them. One thousand years would not be enough time to try to make sense of them. EMDR therapy is not a power think-think session. In this approach to therapy, I'm asking you to do three very basic but central things: activate (but do not overactivate) a piece of a memory, notice what comes to you as a result of that activation, and do this while your nervous system receives a left-right stimulation. The core of this therapy is noticing. Noticing what comes is likely to propel you down the highway toward resolution. The things that you may need to heal might initially appear as a tiny green sign miles away on the interstate. Noticing moves you further and further down the road toward healing. Soon, exactly what you need to heal will come to you like a 30-foot green sign on the side of the road. The difference in EMDR therapy is that you did not construct the sign; you noticed your way to it. What you need to heal will come to you as a byproduct of noticing.

Noticing is the bright yellow line in the center of the road of EMDR therapy. If the client is spending a lot of time doing anything other than noticing, assume that reprocessing probably is not happening in the ways that are most effective and efficient.

Chapter 35
Oh My, Where Do We Start?

It is easy to get overwhelmed by the volume, depth, and wide-ranging impacts and impairments of your client's wounding when you are working with clients who have experienced many of the worst things that humans can experience. A lot of my guidance here is to connect you with the vast amount of information that you already have about working with clients with complex trauma. The odds are excellent that doing Phase One with severely traumatized clients the way you were trained is probably a bad idea since any advantages of conducting a detailed or chronological trauma history are probably not worth the risk of overactivation before the client is prepared to do the work. I don't have clear guidance about where to start with every client, but I have strong recommendations about places not to start. While this chapter does not show you how to make a detailed target selection, it should help you be much more comfortable with the decision to start somewhere and use the information that emerges when you do start somewhere that is both productive and tolerable.

Places Not to Start

Some of the most important memory places that we will need to get to when working with clients with complex trauma are not ideal places to start. As discussed throughout this book, attachment wounds and other targets connected to identity are often the wounds that most broke us when we were children. Also, not consistently getting our needs met usually leaves deficits in adaptive information that directly impair our ability to do EMDR therapy in areas connected with attachment or neglect easily and effectively.

Attachment Wounds

Attachment wounds tend to be the whales of memory for clients who have boats of adaptive information the size of a canoe. Honestly, going fishing for the first time in the ocean and in a canoe is not an advisable thing to do, but with trauma, there is no other way to do it. When clients describe them, attachment wounds do not sound horrible compared to some of the event traumas clients will often report. The client may describe a memory of a Friday afternoon when he was seven years old after the divorce when his father did not come to pick him up. Or she may have had a minor injury playing outside when she was a child and went into the house hoping to get comfort from her mom but was met with anger.

Attachment wounds often sound small, but they are about everything. They are about lovability, safety, trust, belonging, worth, and identity. In short, they are about everything. They are what gets triggered when we have ruptures in our friendships or our intimate relationships. When core attachment wounds clear, enormous amounts of adaptive information appear in the client's nervous system. However, clearing them initially is often a very difficult task without specialized resources in place and the capacity to sit with significant distress for extended periods of time inside, and often outside, of the session.

Because attachment wounds have tentacles that connect to everything and because they connect to some of the most difficult existentially intolerable emotional and somatic states that you are likely to see in EMDR therapy, we need to get there, but it is not advisable to start there.

Identity Targets

As with attachment wounds, targets that connect to many forms of identity (gender, sexual, etc.) are essential targets to explore and resolve, but they are very difficult places to start in the first few reprocessing sessions. Again, they connect to everything. While many clients may have some adaptive information present, much of what is wounding in these experiences often connects to issues of family and cultural judgment, rejections, and externally projected shame that is held internally. In short, these themes are essential for the client's recovery and for living a less encumbered and fuller life. They are particularly complex places to start.

Body Image Targets

It may be tempting to start with body image targets as more tolerable than other targets. However, they are shame-saturated. They are places that we need to get to, but they can be particularly difficult places to start.

Memories Where the Client Is the Abuser

Memories where the client is the one who caused harm to others often requires an abundance of adaptive information (and may require that other forms of healing have already occurred). Memories like this are common in addiction contexts, where the client may have lied, stolen, or worse to source resources for their addictions. Similarly, memories related to wartime behaviors in which others were severely injured or killed because of a client's action or inaction are difficult places to start. In general, event traumas are good places to start if the client isn't the "bad guy" in the bad memory.

First or Worst of Anything

Shapiro is correct in arguing that the first or worst memory in a theme is likely to be the most productive place to work with generally healthy people. This suggestion assumes that clients have a big enough boat of adaptive information to land a memory that is as large as the very first target in EMDR therapy. Shapiro is also clear that it is advisable to start with a very small "test" memory to help clients get familiar with the tasks of EMDR therapy and to help clients develop confidence in this approach generally. She also offers a broad range of alternatives to starting with first or worst, including working on more recent or more tolerable memories. She also suggests ways that interacting with the memory in smaller and more discrete chunks can be helpful.

In short, I rarely start work with clients in the reprocessing phases using the first or the worst of any theme or any "bucket" of client wounding. I want the client to have a good initial experience in EMDR therapy. I have never regretted starting with a "small" memory. I have often regretted when clients start with memories that are too large in the first few sessions. Again, Shapiro was originally obsessed with showing that EMDR therapy is both effective and highly efficient. When starting to work with a client with complex trauma, my focus is on preparing the client to start somewhere, never on developing a plan for getting the client through therapy in the absolute minimum number of sessions possible. The danger of not starting somewhere is that we may not ever start anywhere. I anticipate that clients with severe trauma will be in my caseload for years, even working effectively and efficiently in EMDR therapy.

Shapiro's focus on starting with the first and worst (and most training programs' obsession with it) is largely a testament to the broad health of the people with whom Shapiro developed EMDR therapy. Starting with the first or worst of anything in EMDR therapy is rarely advisable with clients with the complexity that most community mental health therapists encounter unless you have to. However, as we will see below, sometimes you have to.

Start by Starting Somewhere

The remainder of this chapter contains some of the most important ideas that I know about how to communicate when working with clients with complex trauma. The ideas and metaphors aren't just incredibly simple; they should resonate strongly with everything that you already know about working effectively with clients with complex trauma, regardless of how you have worked.

What does being prepared to do trauma work mean? Some consultants suggest that we should prepare clients enough so that they can handle and process their largest memories, should the client's associative memory network take them there. My suggestion is that we prepare clients enough to be able to start somewhere. Starting somewhere allows us to start. If the client hooks a small fish, is it possible that a large shark might bite the fish? Then we have a shark to deal with? Yes, but that is not inevitable, and there are concrete things we can do to help prevent it from happening. Starting somewhere allows us to start building more of the adaptive information needed to eventually digest the larger memories since adaptive information is generated with the resolution of every smaller memory.

Work at the Intersection of Productive and Tolerable

I suggest that in any given session, we target memories that are at the intersection of what is productive and what is tolerable on that day. Productive means that the client would receive a clear benefit from working on it. Productive could also mean that the resolved memory would support current stability. Working on the memory could be productive if its resolution is likely to resolve more than itself (meaning it is representative enough to generalize to other adjacent memories). Tolerable means that the client can handle it today. In the first few sessions, we focus more on tolerable and place less emphasis on productive to help select memories that feel more easily digestible today. How do we select a memory that is productive and tolerable? Have a conversation with the client about it. Therapy is a collaborative endeavor.

Clients with complex trauma will confound our best efforts to overly organize their recovery.

The paragraph above describes how I generally help clients select targets for EMDR therapy. I work at the intersection of what is productive and tolerable. I don't let anyone give me crap about it. If you have worked for hundreds or thousands of hours prior to your EMDR therapy training with clients with complex trauma, I will simply suggest that this is how you have worked when you were working effectively with complex clients. Broadly, I can't imagine a better or more effective way to work with these clients. Is working this way going to take a while? Yes, it will. Every way that is effective will. The territories covered by productive and tolerable may change from week to week, depending on the type of week that your client had and the amount of energy that they have today. That is also okay.

Maybe so much of the confusion about where to work in EMDR therapy comes from the strict training guidance to work with the first and worst when so much of our own sound clinical understanding of complex trauma suggests that this is a terrible place to start with these clients. Again, what you deeply know about working with your complex clients should highly inform how you do EMDR therapy with these clients. There is nothing you should forget about this population to work effectively with it in EMDR therapy. We match our interventions to the unique and complex nervous systems of our clients. Again, EMDR therapy is not a machine we cram people into.

I appreciate that the are many ways to do client history and select initial targets with clients with complex trauma. It is possible that my approach of selecting memories at the intersection of productive and tolerable on any given day might not be the best or most efficient approach in every case with complex clients; I remind myself of what this orientation allows clients to do with great reliability. It allows most complex clients to start this work in ways that are tolerable. Starting reprocessing is one of the most perilous parts of EMDR therapy. It allows clients to resolve increasingly larger memories and build more adaptive information as they go. It allows clients to eventually resolve their touchstone memories with much less disturbance and a much lower risk of decompensation than if we had attempted to begin our work there. It allows healing to happen in every reprocessing session in ways that meet clients where they are on that day. Even if there might be more effective ways to work, this is an incredibly humane way to work. What are other therapists at your agency, in your city, or in your state doing with these clients that is more effective than helping clients with complex trauma regularly and tolerably resolve memories? I suggest that with your clients with pervasively traumatized nervous systems that you work at the intersection of what is productive and what is tolerable, and don't let anyone give you crap about it.

Mount Everest Metaphor

The Mount Everest metaphor is a companion to the Boat and the Whale metaphor covered elsewhere. EMDR therapy connects stuck information to right-now existing adaptive information. The client needs to have enough of the needed adaptive information to be accessible for the difficult information to connect to and be metabolized into. Just like you can't land a whale of a memory into adaptive information the size of a canoe, you cannot metabolize a piece of trauma the size of Mount Everest into adaptive information the size of a walnut.

Shapiro strongly suggests that we work with mountains first, since everything after that will feel like a hill (Shapiro 2018, p. 72). She is correct if the client is an Olympian. My clients are not Olympians. And there are 200 dead bodies on Mount Everest right now. It's not safe to remove them. If our complex trauma clients need to work on traumas the size of Mount Everest (and they probably do), the safest and most sensible strategy is to tackle some hills and some smaller mountains first to build the skills and resources needed to work at that intensity.

Marathon Metaphor

Few of us could run a marathon today. If I had to run a marathon today, I would almost certainly injure myself trying. However, I could start a "Couch to 2K" program that will begin with walking and some jogging. Within a few weeks, I could probably run a 5K (although it wouldn't be pretty). After a few weeks or months of running 5Ks, I could probably run a half marathon. After a few months of running half marathons, I could probably run a marathon. This is what starting somewhere allows. It allows us to get to our goal. But rarely can we start with our goal with complex trauma. Rarely is it required that we be able to.

Sometimes We Have to Start With Mount Everest First (But Rarely)

While it is not a good idea to start with memories the size of Mount Everest, sometimes we are forced to. Sometimes Mount Everest is the mountain that obscures everything else. If the client is going through a gut-wrenching separation or divorce, there probably isn't going to be another target. If the client recently experienced the death of a child, there probably isn't going to be another target. Yes, there are times when we have to start with a larger-than-advisable memory sooner than we would like. When the circumstance requires that we work in this way, I am careful to help the client cut the memory into more tolerable pieces, help calibrate expectations related to rapid progress with the memory, or suggest other accommodations to help facilitate the linkage of adaptive information as tolerably as possible.

Some Suggestions for More Tolerable Places to Start

My clients have generally had good luck starting in some of these territories first. This is not an exhaustive grouping, but it should give you ideas of places to start with most clients with complex trauma.

Phobias

Clients generally do well with tackling specific phobias in EMDR therapy. Snakes, mice, and spiders are good places to start. The phobia of flying in an airplane (with floatbacks and future templates) is productive. Avoid death phobia; it is many-tentacled, and every branch connects to an existentially hard truth.

The Endings of Past Intimate Relationships

It can be productive to start reprocessing around the end of a past intimate relationship several relationships ago. These tend to be tolerable targets because most parts of the client understand that the relationship is objectively over and because relationships tend to end for reasons. Also, wounding connected to the ending of past intimate relationships, while a "normal" part of development, tends to be deeply salient and potentially traumatic. Even if we are happy in a current intimate relationship, we probably got there through various forms of massacre. It may be helpful to explore past intimate relationships as an initial place to work because they may be squarely at the intersection of productive and tolerable. There are some past intimate relationships that are Mount Everest and are not tolerable right now.

Accidents in Which No One Was Seriously Hurt

Car or other accidents in which no one was seriously hurt tend to make good initial targets. Twisted ankles that turn into broken ankles tend to make good starting points for many clients. I like accidents as initial targets because they are discrete events, and they do not generally float back to attachment wounds.

Bad Bosses, Bad Teachers, Bad Peers, or Bad Professors

Is there some relational trauma that does not float back to attachment wounds? Most of us have had ridiculous bosses at some point, and working on some of those memories can be productive. Did the client have any really bad teachers (don't start with those who were physically or sexually abusive)? Childhood bullying, when that is not one of the core life wounds, tends to be a good place to start. Third- and fourth-grade girls can be some of the cruelest people on the planet, yet it was a while ago, so some of it may have settled. Many people who have attended college have had difficult encounters with professors that can make good initial targets.

Any Isolated Event

Event traumas generally make more tolerable targets than non-events or memories that are largely built around absences or neglect. Try to avoid events that connect to attachment wounds as initial targets. I realize that this is easier said than done. Sometimes starting with the memory of "the guy who pulled out in front of me in traffic two weeks ago" makes a good enough initial target. If the client is in a canoe, starting somewhere will let us test the client's fishing gear before we start trying to hook the fish that fill the client's ocean of memory.

Get Information and Let That Shape What Happens Next

The beauty of starting somewhere is that we immediately get helpful information about the client's nervous system. If a particular target was very easy for the client to resolve, I might recommend memory targets that might be heavier in a subsequent session. If the client struggles on a particular day with a specific memory, I work with the client to excavate the source of the difficulty. That difficulty is the information that will help shape where we work next or inform the resources that we need to strengthen. In EMDR therapy, information comes as a gift. If the client has an elegant EMDR therapy processing session, that is information. If the client has a difficult reprocessing session, that also is information. The art of EMDR therapy is figuring out what this information is communicating about your client's unique and complex nervous system.

Get Out of the Way as Soon as Reasonable

This book is filled with adjustments that you can make to standard protocol. However, part of my goal is for the client's nervous system to eventually get healthy enough so that we can work using standard protocol. Allowing things to connect in an unimpeded way allows the possibility of insight to appear. Working slowly allows the client to experiment with and experience alternatives to the information stored in the bad memories. As soon as the client is working reliably, safely, and effectively in EMDR therapy, I begin considering if the restrictions I initially put into place are still needed for the client. I don't want to introduce any limits on reprocessing that are not necessary, and I don't want to keep any limitation on noticing longer than it is necessary for safe and effective processing.

Chapter 36
The Canaries in the Coal Mine

Much of what I suggest in working with clients with complex trauma is that we work in memory territories that are tolerable for the client. How do we know for sure that working in a particular memory territory is a bad idea today? We can't know for sure. We can generally know, for instance, that attachment wounds are difficult memory territory for most people who carry them. But there isn't a lot that we can know for sure. This chapter points out several helpful indicators that can shape your decision about the tolerability and resolvability of a particular memory on a particular day.

What a VOC of One Means From the AIP Lens

The core of the AIP model is that we are always connecting stuck information into right-now adaptive information. Said differently, we are connecting information that is stored in your nervous system to other information that is already stored in your nervous system. How can we check for the presence of the needed adaptive information prior to working on a target? While not a perfect indicator, the validity of cognition (VOC) in Phase Tree is a clue. If the client reports a lot of distress in the memory but reports a VOC of one, this loosely translates to: "There is no part of me that believes that the positive belief might be true related to this memory." While it is possible that the client may be underestimating the amount of adaptive information or that a different positive cognition might be present enough to eventually resolve that memory, a VOC of one is often worth additional exploration. A VOC of one does seem to be a canary in the coal mine, indicating an absence of the very adaptive information that may be needed for this memory to resolve. While I may not abandon a memory in Phase Three, a VOC of one provides a compelling reason why a memory didn't resolve in the subsequent reprocessing phases when the client was able to activate tolerably and notice deeply in the session. It's always possible that the client simply does not have enough of the needed adaptive information for a memory to resolve. This information about this absence is coming as a gift. We need to use it to help the client develop it by using parts work, promoting different relational experiences in real life, or doing more reprocessing of targets in adjacent but different memory networks where the client can endorse a VOC that is higher than one.

Quickly Checking Who Is Responsible Prior to Working on the Memory

Guilt, shame, blame, and responsibility are a lot of what gives trauma its tar-like stickiness. You are likely to be aware prior to the reprocessing phases of EMDR therapy which of your clients blame themselves for everything that has ever happened to them. This blame is typically a protective response to protect the system from harder truths. The problem in EMDR therapy is that we cannot connect a lie to a lie. The nervous system will not allow it in EMDR therapy.

When the client and I are exploring a memory related to childhood sexual abuse, I may ask the client, "Who is the bad person in the memory?"

The client may say, "I am."

"But how old were you in this memory, and how old was he?" I ask.

"I was five, and he was about fifty," she says.

I ask, "When you get in touch with your most grown-up parts, the parts of you that pays bills and puts gas in a car, what percentage of those parts know that a child isn't responsible for what a grown-up does to a child?"

If the client says "zero" or "nearly zero," I am highly unlikely to suggest that the client works on that memory today in EMDR therapy, but we may work in different memory territories where the client does have some of the needed adaptive information present. Or I may continue to try to support adaptive information related to who is responsible for abuse in childhood during this session if the client is willing to engage in that exploration.

Assessing for Preparedness to Work on an Attachment Wound Memory

Events have a beginning, middle, and end. Attachment wounds are about everything. As indicated earlier, be careful starting with attachment wounds before good attachment resources are in place or until adequate parts work has been done. But if the wounding is pervasive enough, there may not be any other accessible targets that don't intersect with the existential abandonment and loneliness of childhood.

Much of the healing that happens in EMDR therapy around attachment wounds occur on a bridge of empathy where information from the most resourced client parts metabolizes the memory information brought by the child parts. How does EMDR therapy work when the most grown-up parts deeply hate, resent, and blame the child parts for what was done to it or for what the child parts did to try to get their needs met? It doesn't. If the most grown-up client parts and the client's kid parts share the same lies, it is unlikely that EMDR therapy around these targets will be productive. Parts work, perspective-taking exercises, psychoeducation, cognitive interventions, and working in different but adjacent memory territories in EMDR therapy can all be helpful.

As explained in the parts work sections, the following questions are helpful to assess if enhanced attachment resources may be needed:

- When you were young, who was really and consistently there for you?
- When you think about yourself at five, six, or seven years old, how do you feel about yourself? Do you feel a deep empathy, or do you blame or resent that child?
- Can you notice what happens in your body when you imagine the most grown-up parts of you being in the same room with the child parts of you?
- Can you notice what happens in your body when you imagine the most grown-up parts of you giving a hug to a child part of you?

When Clients Want to Work With the Biggest Monsters First

In many thousands of EMDR reprocessing sessions with my clients, I remember four sessions as the most distressing, intense, and dysregulated sessions I have ever observed in EMDR therapy. Two of those four were with clients who insisted on working with their touchstone memories during the first or second reprocessing sessions. In both cases, I clearly and strongly recommended that we start somewhere else. Both were prepared to start work in EMDR therapy. Both had attachment resources in place. I gave sound reasons why working on memories that large are likely to cause more problems than they solve and why it makes better sense to start with some smaller things first. I used the Marathon metaphor and the Boat and the Whale metaphor. Both insisted that they were prepared to work on a memory this size. They were not. In addition to a horrible response in sessions, both reported significant decompensation in the days following those difficult sessions.

If I had to do it again, I wouldn't change much. I told both of these clients at the beginning of their therapy with me that I'm not confused about whose therapy this is. I explained that therapy is a collaborative process and that their input is essential. I also communicated clearly what my concerns were with their plan. What I did not tell you in the story above is that I have probably had hundreds of sessions with other clients who indicated that they wanted to work in memory territory that I believed was probably too big to start with in EMDR therapy. Do you know what happened in those cases? Nothing dramatic. In many cases, my intuition was right, and the client agreed after a few sessions to pivot to more tolerable areas for a while. In other cases, the clients cleared their memories in a session or two.

I am discussing this topic in this section because EMDR therapy often does not play well with agendas that are too heavy. When either the client or the therapist brings too strong or too heavy of an agenda, the agenda may force us to look at the world through a straw and prevent access to the broader view that may be needed for actual healing to occur.

Why Overactivation Is a Problem in EMDR Therapy

In EMDR reprocessing phases, we need distressing content to come, but it needs to come into awareness in tolerable pieces and at digestible rates. It is important to recognize that distress with clients with complex trauma doesn't want to come into awareness at measured rates. It is crucial to realize that many of our clients have a baseline traumatic load that significantly impairs their window of tolerance. Activating, but not overactivating, memory content is a skill that we need to develop in clients who present at sessions with very narrow windows of tolerance.

On the most fundamental level, we are always connecting stuck information with existing adaptive information in EMDR therapy when client are working effectively. The more activated a client is, the more salient and true the maladaptive beliefs feel. Also, many forms of adaptive information "live" in the most adult or grown-up parts of the client's system. These are the parts that, hopefully, understand fundamental truths like children are not responsible for what grown-ups do to them. A lot of adaptive information is stored in our neocortex, the part of the brain that tends to get muted when people with complex trauma get overactivated.

In short, overactivation can billow oxygen into the maladaptive fires at the very moment oxygen is being deprived of the parts of the brain that the distress most needs to connect with and be metabolized into. Overactivation typically makes adaptive information less accessible to the system.

Noticing is a bright yellow line in the center of the EMDR therapy road. It's the big center wheel of the metaphorical EMDR therapy tricycle. It is difficult for anyone to notice deeply on the edge of panic. It is difficult to notice distress when distress appears everywhere. Overactivation impairs the most active of the active ingredients essential to recovery in EMDR therapy.

Chapter 37
How We Interact With the Memory Matters

In EMDR therapy, we need memory content to come, but we need it to come into awareness at a digestible rate and a tolerable intensity. The problem is that trauma in people with complex trauma isn't stored in small and discrete packages. It's stored big, and it's felt big. Its lessons and their bodily expressions aren't meant to be ambiguous or experiences subtly. One of the most common places where EMDR therapy breaks down is when too much memory content comes into working memory too quickly. Clients with complex trauma may start with one memory and then many want to come into working memory. I explore in other sections of this book how clients with complex trauma easily pivot from a single memory to a broad theme, and this rarely ends in sunshine. Once trauma hits the body, memories with the same body feel often want to come into awareness as though pulled by the strong magnet of the body state. Another common breakpoint in EMDR therapy is when intense content from a single piece of memory comes into awareness too quickly, like a tsunami. In short, many EMDR therapy sessions with complex clients go sideways as a result of overactivation. Some clients come to sessions with their metaphorical football helmets on thinking that they need to constantly push into or tackle the memory like it is a football sled.

What Exactly Are We Asking Clients to Do in Phase Four?

Most of an average reprocessing session is spent in Phase Four, and the core task I'm asking the client to do over and over is to simply notice what is happening in the nervous system following the last round of activation. When we first arrive in Phase Four using the standard protocol, the part of the memory that the client is noticing was activated in Phase Three. I want the client to notice what has been activated in Phase Three before they activate more. Clients will assume that they should continue playing and activating the memory in Phase Four while they are attempting to notice the last "bite" of activation. This is an invitation to overactivation with clients with complex trauma. That's not what we are asking them to do. We do not instruct them to keep one eye on the bad memory and notice what is happening in the nervous system with the other. I want all of the focus to be on the present activation. I do not want clients to stay focused on the bad memory and also try to notice the activation that has already occurred. Attempting to do both is like trying to mindfully notice while you are standing in the middle of an open doorway to a barn. Horses, cows, and pigs rush out of the barn and run straight into you. With clients with complex trauma, we need to put a gate on the memory channel to help make sure that content is coming into awareness slowly enough to be digestible and tolerable. Remember that the goal of EMDR is to connect stuck information into right-now adaptive information. What happens to adaptive information when we are overactivated? It becomes less accessible (or farther away), and the maladaptive "fires" want to grow.

When we put a gate on the memory channel, aren't we restricting the client's reprocessing and potentially cutting off some channels of noticing that might be helpful? Yes. We can remove any and all restrictions the moment they are no longer needed. However, my goal in each of the first few sessions is to help a client resolve a tolerable memory in a tolerable way and not one thing more. I want the client to experience healing from something. I'm not seeking client insight into how their traumas broadly relate to each other across their lifespan. Insight will come later. I'm trying to help the client heal by processing a cup of gunpowder one spoonful at a time. Or, using a different metaphor, we will briefly open the door or gate on the memory and close it. The client will digest the content that came into awareness when it was briefly opened. When that piece of the memory is digested, I'll direct the client to access the next tolerable piece.

Standard protocol promotes distress coming in as a large wave. Large waves in EMDR therapy require a large window of tolerance, something few clients with complex trauma have. Standard protocol promotes things going anywhere they might want to go. The advantage of bringing smaller pieces of the memory into working memory is that clients with complex trauma will process these experiences faster and with much less distress. Back to the Boat and the Whale metaphor, if we are connected to a large fish, how we interact with the fish matters. It may not be wise or kind to ask the client to stand in a small canoe in the ocean and yank violently until the fish is landed. This is an invitation for snapped fishing lines, flipped boats, or injuries. We want to show the client how to land memories well and with as little unnecessary distress as possible. I want the client to activate some and notice, notice, and notice. Reel the line in a little, let it run, and notice, notice, notice, notice. Reel a little more, let it run and exhaust itself, notice, notice, and notice.

Using a Bean Bag to Activate Digestible Pieces of the Memory

An alternative to going into the memory at the worst part using standard protocol is to do an abbreviated Phase Three (see the Videotape Approach in the next chapter) and use a bean bag or other object to help the client activate smaller "chunks" of the memory. This intervention originally came out of my work with Flash but is very helpful when we need to try to manage overactivation in EMDR therapy.

In standard protocol, we ask something like the following: "When you return to the memory where we started, what are you noticing?"

But in this approach, we say: "Throw the bean bag up into the air and catch it. I only want you to think about the bad memory while the bean bag is in the air." The bean bag serves as a timer that limits exposure to the memory content. Also, in order to catch the bean bag, the client will need to visually track it. Tracking it taxes focus and may help prevent the client from having a flashback or overactivating the memory. As soon as the client finds activation, we ask them to drop the bean bag and notice the activation while engaging in bilateral stimulation. We continue standard rounds of bilateral with noticing, doing check-ins as usual in Phase Four, and not throwing the bean bag again until the last piece of distress has been fully or mostly digested.

The client can progressively throw the bean bag higher as it takes longer to find the next piece of activation. Once the client needs more time to find the activation in the memory than throwing the bean bag allows, return to standard protocol using: "When you return to the memory where we started, what are you noticing?"

This often allows you to process the most distressing parts of the memory by cutting them into smaller and more tolerable pieces.

Do Not Think About the Memory if I Am Not Right-Now Asking You To Think About It

If you are using the standard protocol and the client is struggling with too much activation, another highly effective strategy is to discourage the client from thinking about the memory in Phase Four while they are currently noticing distress. "If you are noticing distress, I want you to notice it and digest it. If you are not noticing distress, I'll send you back to the target memory to see if we can activate some of it for you to notice." Clients will think that they absolutely have to "have one foot in the past and one foot in the present." They do not. For clients with complex trauma, that is one of the most difficult and inefficient ways to do EMDR therapy. I want you to have both feet in the present and I'll send you back to the memory when the last round of distress has been metabolized.

The language I have used for this is: "When I am asking you to notice, and the bilateral stimulation is happening, I do not want you to think about the memory. I do not want you to think about the memory if I am not right-now asking you to think about the memory. Just notice deeply what is happening in your right-now nervous system and digest what has already been activated. When the distress is gone or mostly gone, let me know and I'll send you back to the memory to get more to notice."

Chapter 38
The Videotape Approach

It's not a mystery why Shapiro wants therapists to enter the memory at the worst part. The worst part, when it resolves, is likely to generalize quickly throughout the rest of the memory and cause rapid resolution of the remaining parts of the memory. For really healthy people, the worst part is likely distressing enough to cause enough activation for clients to notice but not too much to saturate them. This is the fastest way to digest a memory when working with healthy clients who have an abundance of adaptive information and a large window of tolerance. Remember, Shapiro was initially obsessed with EMDR therapy as a brief approach to psychotherapy. However, it is nonsensical to think that going into a memory at the worst part is the fastest way through with clients with significant deficits of adaptive information and for clients who come to sessions already nearly outside of their window of tolerance (despite months of work developing and practicing regulation strategies). Standard protocol, including going into the memory at the worst part, is an invitation for overactivation, and much of the remainder of the session may be spent clearing up the tsunami of the flooding that occurred in the first few minutes of a reprocessing session. All of the noticing that is productive in EMDR therapy needs to occur inside the client's window of tolerance. Going into a memory at the worst part with many clients with complex trauma often feels like approaching a large bucket of gunpowder with a lit match. And it's not necessary. We have options for how the client interacts with the memory inside EMDR therapy when starting with clients with severe trauma. Shapiro herself recommends other strategies, one of them is the Videotape Approach. Shapiro did not publish a script for the Videotape Approach but described it as a part of the Recent Events Protocol. My version below revises Phases Three and Four. The other phases are not changed. This is one way to do the Videotape Approach. Drop any elements from the revised Phase Three below that are unnecessarily triggering or that do not resonate with your clients.

Chapter 39
Videotape Approach Script

Revised Phase Three

Parts that are bold, italicized, and in quotes are the parts of the script that you might say to the client. The goal is not to start activating the memory until Phase Four, which is why multiple steps from the standard protocol are skipped in Phase Three and slightly reworded.

Target Memory:

Just make a few notes. Do not have the client tell you much about the memory at all since the goal is to avoid activation in Phase Three.

"The memory that you will be working on today has a beginning and an end. A single memory happens at a particular place at a specific time, and it typically lasts from several moments to several hours (at most). Without playing the memory or thinking much about it, can you quickly identify the beginning of this memory and can you identify a good endpoint to it? Again, a single memory is a single incident and doesn't last days. Just let me know when you have it."

Discourage the client from giving you any details. All you need to know is that he has the beginning and ending point of this piece of video.

"Without thinking much about this memory, is there a negative "I" statement that you associate with it?" You can give examples if that is helpful.

"What would you like to believe about yourself related to this memory?"

"On a scale of one to seven, how true does that positive belief feel right now related to that memory, with one being "I don't believe it at all" and seven being "I believe it fully?"

VOC: _____

Without thinking about this memory in any detail, how difficult or impactful has this memory been on you on a zero to 10 scale over the course of your life, with zero being no distress and 10 being maximum distress?

Again, we're trying to scale the historical intensity or impact of this memory (to get a general sense of how "big" this memory is), not the present distress the client is feeling in this moment related to this memory, since we are not trying to activate just yet.

Generalized Historical SUDs: _____

Revised Phase Four

In a moment, I'm going to ask you to play the memory very slowly, one frame at a time, starting at the very beginning. When you find distress in the memory, simply let me know by raising your hand or nodding. When you find it, I'm going to ask you to close the door on the memory and simply notice the distress in your body. Notice the distress like you would notice an object in the world. Notice its shape, temperature, texture, size, pressure, heaviness, movement, or stillness. In short, notice that sensation like you are about to sketch it. Good. Play the memory very slowly from the beginning and let me know when you find the first piece of distress, even if it's only a little bit. Don't play too much of it. Just let me know. Pause until the client indicates that distress has been found.

Good. Now, see the door on the memory channel close just for now, and don't think about that memory again until I ask you to. Just zoom in and notice the distress in your body as we begin the left-right stimulation.

Do a standard length of 30-45 seconds of noticing with fast bilateral.

Good. Big breath... [allow client's breath to fully finish] What *are you noticing?* [pause]

Notice that or ***Go with that.*** Continue bilateral rounds.

Keep asking the client what he is noticing and going with that with more rounds of bilateral until the right-now body-based distress is declining. Note, you will hear the declining distress in the client's report during the check-in, i.e. "It's getting better," "It's spreading out," "I feel okay." If you cannot tell from the client's report or affect what their level of current body distress is, you can ask them occasionally (not after every set!): ***"How much distress do you have in your body in this moment on a 0-10 scale?"*** If the number is three to four or above, keep doing bilateral sets for 30-45 seconds, pause and breathe, then standard check-in until the current body-based distress is falling into a tolerable range.

If the current body-based distress from the current piece of the memory is decreasing, you should ask the client to play the memory forward and let you know when he finds the next piece of distress: ***"Good. Play the memory forward and let me know with your hand or a nod when you find the next piece of distress."*** When the client finds distress, ask them to close the memory channel and notice the distress. Process this with more rounds of bilateral until the distress activated by this piece is declining (until about a three or less on body-based SUDs... again, do not ask SUDs after every set!).

Keep doing the loop of light activation and multiple rounds of bilateral/noticing until the SUDs for each piece of the memory falls to a tolerable range. We are metaphorically taking small and digestible "bites" out of this memory to help keep the client from overactivating on the memory channel.

At some point, usually after 20 to 40 minutes, the client will arrive at the end of the memory. Repeat the process the same as above until the client gets to the end of the memory again. The client will keep processing in this way, one bite at a time, until there is no distress on any channel and the client is able to play the whole memory all the way through without any distress. Subsequent loops through the memory typically take less and less time.

Then ask, ***"How much distress is in that memory right now on a zero to 10 scale?"*** If there is residual distress when looking at the memory as a whole, continue bilateral processing until the distress is metabolized. If there is no distress, go to Phase Five and resume standard protocol.

Chapter 40
When to Let New Memories In, When to Container

Clients with complex trauma sometimes start with individual memories and then open up a large number of adjacent memories or assorted memories in different developmental eras. If this happens with a relatively healthy client, the best guidance is to stay out of the client's way and let them come. They are likely to resolve all of them in a long string. Again, healthy clients have a boat the size of a cruise ship, and they can generally land whatever they target within a session or two. Allowing a client with complex trauma and little adaptive information to open a large number of memories, especially in the first dozen reprocessing sessions, is not going to end well. Again, we need memory content to come in EMDR therapy, but it needs to come at a digestible rate and intensity.

Why Lots of Memories Want to Come

Memories want to come because there are a lot of them stored tightly in memory networks. Part of what makes complex trauma so complex is that the lessons of it are so redundantly placed. An attachment figure or a family member who has the capacity to be horrible probably has the capacity to be horrible almost all the time and in many different contexts. When any individual memory is activated, even a "small" one, it has a specific body feel. When the body is activated from specific content, similar memories want to come into working memory as though they are pulled by a strong magnet. Additionally, large numbers of similar memories are stored in associated memory networks. Activating one memory can strongly resonate with similar memories.

Clients with complex trauma often pivot from an individual memory to a theme. Themes contain many memories, and these memories may be spread across many developmental eras. This is something that clients with complex trauma also do outside of EMDR therapy. As we will see, when we get activated in EMDR therapy and our bodies start to feel a way that is intense and familiar, we tend to default to the processes and strategies that we do when we are activated outside of EMDR therapy. Our goal in this therapy is to have a disconfirming experience rather than a confirming one. Allowing default processes to execute their functions when they are likely to be overactivating will introduce challenges that are difficult to manage.

It is possible to identify a memory and then put a fence around it to prevent lots of other things from coming in. Yes, this is restricting the clients' processing, but it is often a reasonable restriction early in treatment. Some toddlers need to wobble and bang around a living room to develop independence and competence in navigating the world. Some toddlers will absolutely turn all the gas knobs on or run straight off the nearest cliff. Knowing one from the other allows for better and safer guidance.

Why It's Sensible Not to Let Them In

Our goal in the session is to resolve the memory that we initially selected. We selected the memory on purpose as a reasonable memory to try to metabolize today. Resolving that memory will likely cause multiple adjacent memories to resolve through generalization. Generalization is a process in transformational trauma therapies where memories that are closely networked may resolve automatically without the client needing to actually bring them into working memory. Imagine that a client's uncle was physically abusive 50 times. If these memories are very similar and stored in the same memory network, resolving the first and the worst memory in two back-to-back sessions might automatically resolve 40 or more of them that the client never has to touch. This is part of what is remarkable in transformational trauma therapies. Resolving representative individual memories can resolve many memories that have the same "shape." Metaphorically, the resolution of a memory in EMDR therapy creates a pathway of healing that has a specific shape, and similar memories that share that shape can resolve as a byproduct of the representative memory resolving. However, imagine that an uncle was physically abusive 50 times and while trying to resolve the first memory, the 12th, 15th, 22nd, 31st, and 48th memory of physical abuse from the uncle came into working memory all in a single session. With clients with complex trauma, allowing all of those adjacent memories to come into working memory is almost certain to result with none of them resolving or shifting. The client is also likely to go home with a lot of adjacent memory content activated or smoldering unnecessarily. Resolving a representative memory allows broad general-ization to happen.

The Grill in the Backyard Metaphor

It is important to be strategic about what we target and also be selective about not letting too much memory content come into awareness faster than the client can digest. Imagine that you have a grill in your backyard. You selected the items that you are grilling on purpose. The smells from your grill may spread across your entire neighborhood, and a lot of neighbors may want to come to your barbeque. The denser your neighborhood, the more neighbors you may attract. However, just because they want to come, that does not mean that they should be allowed to barge through your door, walk across your living room, open your sliding back door, and take food off of your grill. It's your grill. It's your door and your living room. You do not need to let in everything that knocks. It makes sense that these other memories want to come. But the door of your awareness is your door. Letting clients know that they do not have to let everything in that knocks may be an opportunity to practice a kind of internal agency and internal boundary that is deeply helpful in trauma recovery. This is why we have the container resource. We cannot work everywhere all at once. In order to work somewhere productively, almost everything else needs to be kept out. The grill metaphor is a good one to share with clients with complex trauma.

A Sensible Decision Tree for Letting New Memory Content In

My suggestion here is that we be careful about what we encourage the client to bring into working memory. However, it is also true that the things that come into awareness in EMDR therapy do so for reasons. I am not suggesting that clients should never let other memories come into working memory, only that we should evaluate if now is a good time for more content to emerge. The following sections are how I help the client make this decision quickly and efficiently about what to do when additional memory content wants to come into working memory.

Check With Me First

I anticipate that many memories will want to come into working memory once the initial target memory is activated. I will explain the Grill in the Backyard metaphor. I let the client know that if a flood of memories wants to come in, simply let me know that is happening, and I can help the client contain them. If a single memory wants to come, I ask the client to simply let me know that it is knocking before he lets it into focus.

Check Time

One of the most important tasks of an EMDR therapist is to always keep track of time. We need to always end sessions in the best way possible and we need to allow plenty of time for closure. If most of the session is over and it is nearly time for closure and another memory wants to come, I ask the client to contain it, and we add it to the list of potential targets. Is there time to notice and digest this content? If not, don't bring it into working memory.

Is the Memory That Wants to Come a Feeder Memory?

I am not convinced that feeder memories as frequent of a problem as EMDR consultants believe they are. Yes, it is possible that a memory may get some of its heat from prior experiences. Later abandonments are built on top of prior ones in cases of complex trauma. Each and every one of them. Almost every memory for clients with complex trauma has floatback memories to some degree, and going all the way back isn't wise when these earlier memories tend to be whales. I see clients with complex trauma resolve memories with extreme regularity, including memories where prior memories set the foundation for the current pathology. Yes, it is better if we could start with the foundational memories. But the dilemma of trying to land the whale into the canoe surfaces again.

There are some memories where nearly all of the distress comes from a prior experience. But in a full-time caseload of clients with complex trauma, it does not happen every day, every week, or even every month. It does happen, though. For instance, a client wanted to target a difficult confrontation with a boss. When we were about five minutes into reprocessing, the client said, "Crap. This isn't about my boss. This is about the time my father said the same thing to me when I was about seven." Clearly, the memory we started with isn't going to resolve until we resolve the memory with the father. However, that does not mean that we *have to* pivot to the earlier memory with the father right now in this session, particularly if we selected the memory of the boss because it was a more tolerable place to start. What did we do? The client and I had a conversation about the wisdom of pivoting to that attachment wound memory with the father today, and we agreed that it was too big of a fish for this session and the client put both of them into a container. We moved to closure and engaged in resources. The client returned to that memory several months later when he had the adaptive information needed to metabolize memories that large with much less effort.

How Are You Handling What You Are Already Hooked To?

Even if there is time in session and another memory wants to come into awareness, I want it to come in at a good time. I realize that we are not checking the SUDs throughout the session, but how is the client doing in this moment? If you were to check the right-now body-based SUDs, would it be seven, eight, nine, or ten? If so, now is not a good time to let new content in if the client is still clearly distressed by the content that they are already connected to. If you are in an eight-foot canoe and you are hooked to a seven-foot tuna, you have your hands full. You will be lucky to land what is already on the line, and we have no business hooking onto another large fish.

As the client becomes more comfortable with EMDR therapy and is resolving memories effectively, it is essential to start removing the initial restrictions that we put in place and allow the client's nervous system to explore other territories and allow additional connections and insights to emerge. However, the ability to pick our battles and pick our adversaries on any given day are essential tasks for doing trauma work well, safely, and in the most efficient ways possible.

Chapter 41
Where Clients Get Stuck and How to Intervene

EMDR therapy can be difficult with clients with complex trauma. However, there is some good and encouraging news. When clients with complex trauma get stuck in EMDR reprocessing, they tend to get stuck in a limited number of places and for a limited number of reasons. A single jet engine on a modern aircraft might contain 35,000 individual parts, and thousands of them might be moving parts. A significant problem in almost any of them could cause problems for the engine and for the flight. The range of problems that occur in EMDR therapy tends to be much simpler. From the lens below, there are less than a dozen places where clients with complex trauma tend to struggle. This lens assumes that several core things are already in place (for example, adequate embodiment, resources, and the presence of adaptive information). Other parts of the book assess deficits in needed preparation skills and other challenges to address prior to reprocessing. This section focuses on the most common places where EMDR reprocessing slows or breaks down (typically in Phase Four) for clients who have adequate resourcing in place.

When They Are Stuck, They Are Stuck Somewhere

When clients have problems inside EMDR therapy reprocessing, they have problems somewhere. It is important to gather as much information as possible to determine where they are actively stuck. Our interventions should match the stuck point. For instance, if you get into your car and your car does not start, it is not helpful to get out of the car and check the tires. We want to strategically intervene where the problem actually is. It will take a while for new EMDR therapists to intuit what is happening and why. This section helps describe what it looks like when clients are stuck in specific places in EMDR therapy, how to intervene, and how to continue work after the intervention.

What Stuck Looks Like

Some new EMDR therapists struggle to understand what EMDR looks like when reprocessing is happening and the client is on the pathway. If the client is not stuck, we need to be vigilant against intervening. Many new trainees are so accustomed to providing help, sharing supportive information, or giving comfort to clients in distress that it can be difficult to adjust to a psychotherapy centered around being present with and noticing distress (especially when that distress is increasing).

If clients are on the path in EMDR therapy, no intervention is needed as long as the client is willing and able to continue noticing within the time available. Some targets will not be resolved in one session. Some targets may not be resolved without the client noticing substantial amounts of distress. Clients may go into some targets expecting a substantial amount of distress and it may resolve with much less distress than was anticipated.

Memories resolve in EMDR therapy when clients are able to activate a piece of difficult memory content (but do not overactivate), notice deeply what is coming up in right-now awareness, and do this while the system is engaging in some form of bilateral stimulation. Central to noticing is activation. EMDR therapists are skeptical of reprocessing sessions where distress is absent. The goal of EMDR therapy is to allow difficult information to link up with and be metabolized into right-now adaptive information. Noticing distress in EMDR therapy is generally distressing for the client. But is the content of the distress changing? Is the distress changing? If so, assume for this moment that reprocessing is occurring. EMDR therapists are comfortable with distress when the content the client is noticing is changing in some way. The ultimate measure of progress is that the memory moves toward adaptive information and resolution.

Clients with complex trauma are often trying to connect significant memories to very limited amounts of adaptive information. Their metabolization rate of this information may be slow. It is often difficult to distinguish between stuck sensations and slowly moving ones. When in doubt, ask. It is better to confirm that the client is actually stuck before intervening than to intervene when things are just moving slowly. When the client says, "It's in my chest," multiple times during check-ins, that information might be ambiguous. It might be shrinking or expanding slowly. It might be pulsing, cooling, or getting hotter. Or it might be stuck-stuck.

After two or three rounds where the client reports that a sensation is not changing, instruct the client to do the following: "On the next round, just zoom into that sensation and notice deeply if that sensation is stuck-stuck, or if there is something changing about it, even if slowly." If the client reports that it is changing, ask the client to notice what is changing during the next round of bilateral stimulation, even if it is changing very slowly. If the client reports that the sensation is stuck-stuck, inquire with the client if they have any insight about why that sensation is getting stuck. Sometimes clients have information that is helpful in selecting the interweave, sometimes they don't. The information that they communicate or information that you might be able to intuit can be helpful for the intervention.

Interventions Are Perspective Changes

What do clients do in EMDR therapy sessions when their bodies feel things that are familiar? They typically use strategies that they use outside of EMDR therapy when their bodies feel this way. They may tend to ruminate, disconnect, actively avoid, try to contextualize by bringing in other instances or memories, purposefully bring in positive self-talk, or fall into the black hole of self-blame or shame. All of these are unlikely to be productive. And again, when clients are stuck, they are stuck somewhere. They are stuck in a perspective that is not currently productive. Of the many things we know about trauma is that it significantly constrains perspective. Trauma is stored in ways and in parts of the brain that are perspective-limiting.

Interweaves invite a change in perspective. If a client is stuck on the thought channel, switching to the body sensation is a channel change, but it is also a perspective change. Imagine a car repeatedly runs into an obstacle head-on, backs up, and then hits that object in the same way over and over. Now, imagine a passenger observing this gets out of the car and surveys the situation. The passenger asks the driver to back up and then turn the wheel as far right as possible. Even if that direction change causes the car to bump into the wall again, it may be enough of a change in perspective to help the car bounce around the obstacle. When the client encounters an obstacle over and over without any change, the therapist must intervene and introduce a perspective change. Being stuck in EMDR therapy is emotionally draining for the client, and allowing them to stay stuck for long periods may promote body sensations that might be difficult to tolerate. It may spread "embers" from the developmental era of that memory that cause severe problems functioning for days after a reprocessing session.

Common Reprocessing Problems From Inadequate Preparation

This chapter does not address every possible problem that may occur if the client is not adequately prepared for the EMDR therapy journey. The sections below divide problems that may occur in Phase Four-Six into two broad categories: problems that emerge primarily because of inadequate preparation and common problems in the reprocessing phases of EMDR therapy once the client is adequately prepared.

The Client Is Not Embodied Enough to Notice

Clients need to be in their bodies enough to notice. If the client is not embodied enough to notice, the client may struggle to activate a memory or everything that comes may be thoughts. Emotions are thoughts about feelings if you are not in your body enough to notice. Trying to do EMDR therapy with clients who are somatically disconnected is usually a goose chase.

The Client Does Not Have Adequate Resources

The EMDR journey for people with complex trauma is much more difficult without solid resources in place. Imagine needing to go on an extensive journey in a car without working brakes, an engine that needs mechanical work, without any money, and with no clear plan of where you are going or where you will stay each night. A journey without adequate preparation to manage what may come up is inherently stressful. Other sections of this book explore enhanced resourcing.

The Client Does Not Have Enough of the Needed Adaptive Information

At its core, EMDR therapy connects old stuck information into right-now existing adaptive information. The needed information must be present and there must be enough of it, or the target memory will not be able to metabolize into it.

The Client Does Not Understand EMDR Therapy

Clients who do not understand what I'm asking them to do inside an EMDR reprocessing session will struggle in many ways. It is helpful to walk them through Phases Three through Eight so that they can see clearly what you are asking them to do at each step and so that different parts of them can give consent to working this way. Clients who do not understand their role in this dance will try to do their job, my job, and the universe's job. I am asking the client to activate a piece of a memory, notice what comes, while their nervous system receives a bilateral stimulation. If the client is doing anything else, they may be stirring green beans into the EMDR brownie batter… and the brownie batter is really good without these additions.

The Client Does Not Have the Capacity to Feel Worse Today

In any given reprocessing session, clients need the capacity to feel worse. If the client is prepared to do EMDR therapy and today is the most anxious or most depressed I have seen him, we will probably not engage in EMDR reprocessing unless we target the event that activated the current mood state. The beginning of an EMDR reprocessing session typically begins with a small or deep dive into noticing distress. Clients need the capacity to feel worse for a while or they will quickly be bumped out of their window of tolerance and struggle to notice in ways that are productive.

Common Reprocessing Problems

Clients with complex trauma who are adequately prepared for the EMDR journey can still struggle with the reprocessing phases. The sections below are places where clients are most likely to encounter difficulties. Please note that this section may not be exhaustive, but it does capture the vast majority of difficulties you are likely to see.

Do The Client's Parts Consent to Working on This Memory?

It is helpful to get consent from client parts to do this work. You can simply ask at the beginning of Phase Three, "Do all parts of you think doing this work is a good idea today?" If not, find somewhere more tolerable to work. If you don't inquire about consent, parts may not allow you to activate or may start somatic side fires to distract from the target memory.

Is the Target an Actual Memory

In Phase Three, you should be careful to make sure that the target is a memory. "Bullying my seventh-grade year" is not a memory. "The thing my mother said repeatedly to me when I was a child" is not a memory. "Why was I born to these people?" and "Why does my mother treat me differently than my sister?" are not memories. If you cannot find an individual memory because trauma was daily and no individual memory stands out, see the subsequent chapter Trouble Finding an Individual Memory When Trauma Was Daily. When the target is not a memory, it is often a broad theme. Clients may have all of the activation that may be common in memory reprocessing, but they will often have very little movement because too much memory content is activated. Part of your psychoeducation about EMDR is that when we are working with the past, we are almost always working on a memory. Let clients know that if they pivot from an individual memory to something else, they should communicate that to you so that you can provide appropriate guidance.

Is the Client Connected to a Whale of a Memory?

When healing happens in EMDR therapy, it does so because the client has been able to connect stuck information into existing adaptive information. For this to occur, the client needs to have enough of the needed adaptive information. Adaptive information is not one thing. Many people may have adequate information in some areas but may have deficits in other categories of information. Shapiro is very clear that there is nothing in the Eight Phase Protocol that will automatically create adaptive information in an EMDR session if it is not already there. Said differently, you do not get a bigger boat of adaptive information just because you are connected to a large fish. The validity of cognition may be another indicator of pervasive deficits in adaptive information if the VOC is one in Phase Three. You may have also heard many of these deficits in how clients talk about themselves and the world. We cannot land a whale into a canoe. Attachment wounds, memories where the client is the abuser or bad actor in the memory, and targets that intersect squarely with any form of identity challenge make difficult initial targets with clients with complex trauma. Clients connected to a memory target bigger than their right-now boat of adaptive information will often have an abundance of distress, but they have no means for that distress to get better. Their distress may peak and be followed by a shutdown response. Their anxiety may peak near panic before we have them disengage. Or they may be stuck in the big existential loneliness that defined so much of that era of childhood.

Clients are often able to answer if this memory has turned out to be bigger than they anticipated. If the client reports that the memory feels like a whale and they have been doing what you are asking them to do, the most sensible thing to do in a session is often to disconnect from it. I will invite the client to bring in an attachment figure if the memory is an attachment wound. We engage in other resources, especially the container, to help store this memory for a later time. I highly recommend that you work at the intersection of what is productive and tolerable. If this memory turns out not to be tolerable, do some more work in territories that are more tolerable and return to this memory later, once the client has had the opportunity to develop more adaptive information. The therapist can assist the client in developing more adaptive information by working on smaller targets (which always generate adaptive information when they resolve) or do other targeted resourcing to address potential deficits in adaptive information when returning to Phase Two.

Is the Client Able to Stay In the Window of Tolerance?

Many problems in EMDR reprocessing reduce to the problem of too much memory content coming into awareness in too short of a period of time. Problems also come from too much memory intensity coming into awareness too soon. Opening many memories or playing too much of a difficult memory can cause content to overtop the client's window of tolerance. Much of the rest of the session may be consumed by dealing with the residue of the client's initial overactivation. We need memory content to come, but we need it to come in tolerable and digestible ways.

Also, remember that we are connecting stuck information into existing adaptive information. Much of the client's adaptive information is likely to be stored in the rational, sensible, and logical parts of the brain and these may be the very parts of the brain that experience decreased blood flow during overactivation. Overaction can impair reprocessing because it may make the needed adaptive information less accessible to the client's system. There are many strategies that are explored in this book to help make sure that memory content and its accompanying distress are coming into awareness at digestible rates and intensities.

Is the Client Having an Energy Crisis?

Noticing distress in EMDR therapy burns energy like a jet engine. Clients may come to sessions with a substantial sleep deficit or with very little accessible energy. They can get stuck in reprocessing when they do not have the energy to be present with the distress generated by the memory. If the struggle appears to be from an energy crisis, you can try asking the client to engage in movement strategies, arrange for the client to connect with a cool drink if available and appropriate, or allow the client to take a short break or a walk to try to generate additional capacity to notice and tolerate distress.

Is the Client Present?

The client may report distress, but is the distress the client is noticing happening in the present? Clients can easily dissociate into the past, but all of the noticing that is productive in EMDR therapy always happens in the present moment and the right-now body. The client needs to be present enough to notice. If the client is dissociating into the memory, is ruminating, or is not otherwise present enough, invite the client to ground and remind the client that all noticing that is productive happens in the present moment. Ask them to let you know when they lose connection with the present moment. Invite them to bring into sessions whatever they need to try to stay grounded and present.

Grounding skills for clients are essential. The time to teach them is way before the client needs these skills inside an EMDR reprocessing session.

Is the Client Actually Noticing?

The client may be aware of distress, but are they noticing it? Can you think of a time in the past few months when you may have been aware that you were angry or frustrated? Awareness can be a general summary of an emotional state. Noticing is an active verb in EMDR therapy. You may have been aware of anger, but did you notice that your jaw muscles were tight or that you had a warmth in the center of your chest? If clients are activated (or stuck), are they noticing deeply and specifically where they are activated, or do they just have a general awareness of it? If the activation feels stuck, I will verify that the client is stuck, and I will also invite the client to notice deeply where they feel stuck. I will use the instruction: "Scan your body and find the place of most [anger, or whatever the client uses to describe it] and just notice it deeply there for a set of bilateral stimulation. Don't try to change it or fix it, just notice it deeply. Is it hot, cool, heavy, round, or blobby? Does it have a texture or a color or any other quality? Notice the place of most distress like you are about to sketch or draw it."

Again, you are not stuck until you are noticing deeply where you are stuck and it is not moving, shifting, or changing in any way when you notice it.

Is the Distress Where the Client Is Stuck From the Memory?

It is entirely possible that the client may be stuck somewhere other than in the activated content of the memory they identified in Phase Three. Imagine if the client is working on a recent breakup with a partner. The client may start reprocessing with the memory and then get deeply stuck in the existential questions of: "Why does everyone I have ever loved end up hurting me on purpose?" or "Will I ever find love that doesn't end horribly?" Memory content may often pivot to territories other than the memory we selected as the target. If the client is stuck in a territory other than the memory, you can always ask the client to contain where they are stuck and return the client to the target memory.

Is Memory Content Coming into Awareness Faster Than Can Be Digested?

We need memory content to come into awareness in EMDR therapy, but we need it to come at digestible rates. Clients with complex trauma have many memories stored in single memory networks. Many of these memories have the same feeling as the nearby ones. When the client activates a memory in a memory network, the body feels a specific way. The activation from the memory identified in Phase Three can cause many adjacent memories to want to come into awareness because they have the same body feel. See Chapter 40: When to Let New Memories In, When to Container. It is helpful to let clients with complex trauma know that working on one memory at a time is often the best approach, especially when working on the first handful of memories in EMDR therapy.

Is Memory Content Coming Into Awareness With Too Much Intensity?

We need memory content to come into awareness, but it needs to come at an intensity that is within the client's window of tolerance. Anticipate that many clients with complex trauma will begin most sessions with very small windows of tolerance. If distress comes into awareness and overtops the window of tolerance, the client may experience panic symptoms (which will make noticing effectively very difficult) or may have a deep shutdown response that is taking the client offline like an electric circuit breaker that has experienced too much amperage. See Chapter 38: Videotape Approach and Chapter 37: How We Interact with the Memory Matters chapters.

Is the Client Stuck in Guilt, Shame, Blame, or Responsibility?

Conceptually, there are two types of guilt, shame, and responsibility. One is appropriate and one is inappropriate. If I drink too much and punch a friend in the nose and I feel guilty about that, my job in EMDR therapy is to notice that guilt. That memory will not resolve using the cognitions of "I did the best I could," or "I didn't do anything wrong." If it resolves, it will resolve using cognitions like: "I can support my recovery," "I can make better decisions," or "I can try to mend my relationships." Context often comes in and is helpful in reaching some form of adaptive resolution. In this scenario, the way through is to notice it deeply.

Inappropriate guilt, shame, blame, and responsibility are common in memories of childhood sexual abuse. Clients will often get stuck in these lava-hot emotions; they do so largely because the most grown-up parts probably still blame and resent the child states in the memory for not making different decisions or not knowing how to protect themselves. The sections on attachment resources can be helpful in developing and supporting the needed adaptive information so that guilt, shame, blame, and responsibility can be attached where they belong.

Is the Client Trying to Figure Out the Trauma?

EMDR is not a power think-think session with bilateral stimulation. Many clients with complex trauma have attempted to solve the problem of trauma by thinking about it or ruminating about it. Clients whose strategies outside of the session involve excessive thinking or ruminating can probably identify very few (if any) times when these approaches were helpful. Why would we think that they would be helpful with the bilateral stimulation in EMDR therapy? The most prominent element of EMDR timewise is noticing. Noting what is coming and figuring things out are two completely different processes much of the time. It is helpful to remind clients at the beginning of an EMDR session that "there is nothing to figure out today. Whatever you need to heal may come to you as a byproduct of noticing. Can you ask the parts of you that really want to try to figure everything out simply if they would be willing to be curious about what is coming into awareness when you interact with the memory?" See Chapter 34: There Is Nothing to Figure Out Today.

Chapter 42
The Quicksand of Attachment Wound Targets

We are not born into the whole world. We are born into tiny fiefdoms where the adults either know how to love us and care for us well and consistently, or they do not. When I ask clients "when you were young, who was really and consistently there for you?" and they respond with "no one," they do so within about half of a second. The nervous system has already calculated this math. It's one of the truest things they already know. What does it mean to be born into need, but not to be able to get your needs met? It usually means that you were lonely. The most intractable emotion I see that completely stalls reprocessing of attachment wounds isn't anger, sadness, fear, or grief. It is existential loneliness that occurs in the first few sessions when tackling the initial attachment wound memory directly. When this loneliness defined the center of our client's childhood, every subsequent wound is usually a sideshow to this central wound.

Attachment wounding is about everything. It's about lovability, belonging, family, safety, identity, and worth. It's why our relationships are so complicated now. It's the center of most of our insecurities. It's what gets triggered in our adult lives when things upset us. Attachment wounds are the whales of memory. Clients often do not get pervasively healthier until we are able to rescue the child from that horrible childhood loneliness and the meanings that have become attached to it. Attachment wounds are notoriously difficult initial targets in EMDR therapy, but subsequent attachment targets do get easier to resolve once the initial attachment memories resolve.

What "Stuck" in an Attachment Wound Looks and Feels Like

In this chapter, I want to describe a particular type of "stuck" that I have seen hundreds of times. I'm describing it so that you may be able to quickly identify it when it occurs so that you can strategically intervene to help clients better navigate it. When working on an attachment wound, clients access the memory and reprocessing begins. Often, they are able to notice distress, and noticing that distress deeply may cause sensations to move, shift, or change in some ways for a while. Clients may describe the sensation that they are noticing as sad or lonely. However, the bodily sensation starts to fill their bodies, push outside their bodies, and fill the room, the town, and all of the universe. Clients report that they notice "nothing." Sending them back to the target returns "nothing." You (the therapist) may feel uneasiness in your nervous system, especially if the feeling the client is experiencing is personally familiar to you. Your attempts to intervene are not productive. You pivot to closure, and the client reports that they are able to do the exercise, but they continue to report that they are noticing "nothing," and the resources don't seem to be very helpful. This session does not feel right to you, but the "nothing" that they report isn't overtly distressing. They return to the next session and report that they had a horrible experience that lasted for multiple days. They may report that they don't think that they can continue to do EMDR therapy. What happened?

In short, the client may have drilled into the same big existential loneliness that defined much of childhood. That huge loneliness became activated and the client did not have enough adaptive information present in other parts of the system to connect to it and metabolize it. The client's nervous system was flooded with loneliness and that flooding also pushed any potential adaptive information farther away, making it less accessible. Much of our needed adaptive information is often, but not always, held in our most adult (neocortex) parts, and these are the parts that tend to go offline when we are flooded with almost any strong adverse emotions that are intense. This is what I mean when I say that attachment wounds are the whales of memory and that clients with complex trauma begin EMDR therapy with a boat of adaptive information the size of a canoe. This is one of the categories of memory that we often cannot resolve by cutting it into really small pieces or moderating how the client is interacting with the memory (as in the case of the Videotape Approach). This type of memory is most easily resolved in EMDR therapy by making the client's boat of adaptive information bigger. One of the best ways to do that is through parts work. A well-developed attachment figure resource is a good way to help the client develop the needed information to eventually process the memory.

Chapter 43
Understanding the Developmental Deficits of Attachment Wounds

If event trauma causes fractures, attachment wounds cause compound fractures. It is deeply wounding to be born into this world with non negotiable needs and not be able to get those needs met. Parents who do not know how to effectively and consistently meet the needs of a child will often blame and humiliate a child for having those needs. Children learn important things that are essential for healthy development when they are able to get their core needs met. There are significant developmental and informational deficits from not being able to get our needs met, and these deficits can directly affect the fund of accessible adaptive information. These informational and experiential deficits that emerge from unmet need set the foundation for subsequent wounding, insecure attachment, physical health challenges, continued unmet needs in many other domains, and substantial difficulty healing using almost all forms of psychotherapy.

The best way to have a lot of adaptive information is to have had a great childhood and life. In short, life prepares some people very well for EMDR therapy. It also prepares them not to need it. It gives healthy people only a few big things to work on, a broad window of tolerance, and a huge fund of deep and adaptive beliefs about themselves that difficult experiences can easily find and be metabolized into. EMDR therapy is like a magic wand for pervasively healthy nervous systems. Healthy people rarely come to therapy for reasons that are obvious. For clients whose systems hold nearly no adaptive information (who never had the opportunity to have the disconfirming life experiences needed to develop it), there is no magic in EMDR therapy. None. We have to help them create the needed adaptive information, if we would like to work in EMDR therapy. And we have to create it from almost nothing.

What Parts Work Does

It is really difficult to believe that you are lovable if you were not valued and loved by others when you were young. It is easy for a therapist to tell a client that they are lovable. Clients need to viscerally experience it. It is difficult to understand human needs when the people who raised us do not understand who is responsible for meeting those needs. We can clearly tell clients the truth about human needs and who was responsible for meeting them, but this information cannot be easily metabolized in the nervous system until they have deep and somatic experience of it. Experiences metabolize information and make the information actionable. When we are wounded relationally, we need to heal relationally. We can't simply send profoundly wounded clients out into the world to have different relational experiences when they have the same nervous system that has been replicating and reenacting their childhood dynamics. They will likely have retraumatizing experiences. Parts work allows clients to have internal relational experiences moderated by the therapist that can be deeply disconfirming and healing. For some clients with profoundly wounded nervous systems, parts work is their first deep experience with self-compassion, effective self-communication between parts, and deep empathy across developmental eras. Parts work allows easier communication across parts and across developmental eras (which EMDR therapy often requires). In short, parts work provides the experiences that allow adaptive information to be inserted into the client's nervous system and for tentative information to be strengthened.

The Attachment Figure Resource is a Parts Intervention

A well-developed and well-practiced attachment figure resource (see Phase Two section) can be instrumental in helping clients end sessions in ways that are okay while simultaneously modeling the type of nurturing connections that I hope the client will be able to replicate between his parts soon.

Attachment figure resources are one of the few resources I have seen that can decrease the body-based level of distress from 7-10/10 to 1-3/10 within a few moments of bringing it in. Attachment resources can be healing to stuck information and experiences, as they often bring powerful experiences that disconfirm the expectations in the bad experiences of childhood.

A well-developed attachment figure resource models what the client may not be healthy enough yet to do: self-nurture, self-inform, and self-soothe. A large amount of healing happens on a bridge of empathy between parts. Some of the client's first instances of a nurturing connection across developmental eras and between disconnected parts occur in our initial attachment figure resource interventions. Of course, attachment figure resources are just one way to do parts work. The client can accomplish many of the same goals using other approaches to parts work.

Chapter 44
Why Finishing Things Matters in EMDR Therapy

In EMDR therapy and any other therapy with clients with complex trauma, we don't want to make the perfect the enemy of the good. Good is good. If a client's SUDs from a difficult memory decreases from 8/10 down to 2/10, that is good. Whatever remains of that difficult memory will likely be held in a much more tolerable and potentially less damaging way. However, our goal is not simply to decrease distress in an individual memory. It is for the client's pervasively traumatized nervous system to largely reset over the course of treastment. For broad healing to occur, we need to leverage generalization. Generalization occurs when clients resolve things, and the resolution of a single memory instantly results in many similarly linked memories spontaneously resolving. Fully resolving a memory transforms it from support for a negative schema to core support for a positive schema. Part of our goal in resolving the initial sets of memories is to generate more adaptive information that may be needed for larger traumatic memories to be resolved.

Clients, however, will often insist that a partially resolved memory is "good" and that there are much more pressing topics to focus on in subsequent sessions. The therapist may face the dilemma of wanting to return to finish work that the client has little motivation to finish. To be fair, clients are not wrong. They probably do have current concerns that feel much more important than cleaning out any residue from the partially resolved memories of prior sessions. When clients present at sessions with topics that they would like to work on, yet we have multiple unresolved memories, I simply share the dilemma with the client. I may say something like the following:

> We can work in the territory that you would like to work on today, but it's my job to also point out that there are multiple memories that are not fully resolved from recent sessions. Fully resolving a memory clears many other memories that you will never have to touch directly in EMDR therapy. Resolving those memories may make it easier to do the

work that you want to do today and in later sessions. It is okay to have a few partially resolved memories, but it is also important to come back and finish them. Do you have ideas about when we can return to them?

With some younger clients, I may use the Video Game metaphor. I explain the following:

In a video game, we don't simply walk past gold bars and other important resources that we will need for the journey. In each stage of the process, we need to extract the assets that are present in this layer of the game for use in later stages. We don't rush toward the boss fight as fast as we can, or we may find that we don't have the strength, health, or recovery assets needed to be successful when we get there.

Alternatively, I may use a tunnel analogy with some clients:

When a memory fully resolves, it's like a tunnel of information that allows other information to flow. Imagine a tunnel from France to England under the English Channel that is complete except for the last two miles. We may have done really good work. Other projects may demand our attention. However, when the tunnel is complete, a lot of good things can transit through that passageway for decades. It is okay for construction to be delayed, but we don't want to miss the opportunity to finish a project that can help bring supplies needed for future projects on both sides of the channel.

Chapter 45
EMDR Therapy and Grief

There are shelves of sensible, helpful, and well-reasoned books and articles about EMDR therapy. Decades of solid research and scholarship exist about grief. However, much of what I have heard consultants say about EMDR therapy around grief topics goes against every sensible understanding that we have about either. These are just a few examples of the nonsense:

- "It is recommended to wait six months to a year before starting to target anything related to death or grief."
- "You want to give the natural grief processes time to do their thing before you start messing with it with EMDR therapy."
- "We have to wait until the person is completely sure that their loved one is gone before we can start EMDR therapy."

EMDR therapy does not spare us the need to grieve. We grieve by grieving. Often, that is a lifelong process. However, EMDR therapy can help remove the obstacles to adaptive and effective grieving. Guilt, shame, blame, and responsibility are like tarps pulled over grief that can make the grieving process both stuck and eternal.

Grief also appears in many forms not connected with someone's death. Grief is ubiquitous in heartache. We grieve futures that we planned but cannot have. Grief, in all its forms, ensures that we suffer in this life. If you have a really great life and live long enough, everything that you loved when you were young will start to die away. That's wounding. Live long enough and your body and mind will start their long and slow estrangement from you.

One of my first EMDR therapy clients was a man in his 60s whose mother received in-home hospice services about 20 years prior. The client reported that he cried violently almost daily since his mother passed away. His grief was debilitating. In describing the loss, he said, "My mom was sleeping and I laid down to take a little rest. I heard something and I didn't know what it was. I thought it probably was my house air conditioner turning on. I got up a little while later and found that my mom died. I always think that if I had just gotten up my mom would still be alive today." This client was an otherwise intelligent, insightful, and generally self-aware person. Because of the way that this loss was experienced, the client was not able to start the adaptive grieving process because of how he was stuck in blame and responsibility.

In this client's EMDR reprocessing of his mother's passing, the client noticed substantial distress in the memory and arrived at: "My mother was in hospice." This realization appeared as though it was the first time it deeply occurred to him.

Then, "My mother was really sick. She was never going to live more than a few days."

Followed by, "I took care of her the best way I knew how to."

And finally, "I didn't kill her." The client noticed that. Then, huge tears flowed. The client reported that they were good tears. They were the tears that he had not been able to cry before. This was the beginning of the client's adaptive grieving process twenty years after the loss. EMDR therapy helped remove the obstacles to adaptive grieving. These were things that many people had told him, but EMDR therapy allowed him to finally make that information actionable with this loss.

The ease with which clients turn "I might have done something different" into "I killed her" is remarkable. Clients whose family members undergo a doctor-recommended surgery and do not survive the surgery, are often stuck in "I should have made them not do the surgery," which is held by the nervous system as "I killed him." Clients who did not visit an elderly grandparent often enough become convinced that their "neglect" helped kill their loved ones.

Grief is particularly complicated when our relationships are complicated. My mother passed away a few months ago after falling in our house. I had done enough of my own EMDR work related to my childhood traumas to be able to take care of her as her health began to fail several years ago. She was diagnosed with dementia, and it was progressing rapidly the last few months before she fell. On the day she fell, she was not feeling well. She collapsed and fell several times earlier. I was there to catch her each time. She agreed to get in bed and said that she would not get out of bed. When I left the room, she got out of bed and collapsed and fell again. This time she fell into a dresser and broke her neck in multiple places. Because of the underlying state of her dementia, the ER and consult staff did not believe that she would be able to undergo the surgery and participate in the rehab that would be required for recovery. They recommended hospice care, and she went directly from the ER to inpatient hospice. Hospice gave her enough pain medication to keep her comfortable. This is what she wanted. It was also enough medication to keep her from eating or drinking. She did not die from a neck fracture. She died from malnutrition. This was horrible to witness. I witnessed as much of it as I could, which wasn't as much as I should have. It took ten days for her to die. In many ways, she died a comfortable and "natural" death. It was a complicated death, and images of her slowly sliding into it were stored in the part of my brain where trauma is stored. I felt the pull of guilt, shame, blame, and responsibility. I should not have left the room before she fell. Part of me knew that she would not stay in bed. Was I too quick to agree to hospice? Taking care of her was more exhausting than I realized when I was in it. She had been up for hours at a time in the middle of the night before she fell. She regularly turned on the faucets and forgot to turn them off. When she was up, I had to be also. When she was dying in hospice, the house was still and quiet all night for the first time in months. I realized I slept the whole night through. Parts of me were afraid that she would die before more family members could arrive in town to say goodbye. Parts of me were terrified that she wouldn't die.

Many people in my generation are trying to figure out how to take care of people who didn't know how to take care of them in the 1970s and 1980s. When she was dying, I also had flashbacks of lovely memories. I felt myself as a little child holding tight to a piece of her flowing skirt as we were moving through a store in about 1973. I remembered how happy she was on a particular day in August of 1990. Parts of me were already missing her. And in a single moment, you lose both mothers. You lose forever the one you had. You also lose all hope for the one you always needed.

Loss can be traumatic for those of us still here. It has the potential to get stuck in places where trauma is stored. Parts of it can get stuck and serve as a bottleneck that prevents us from accessing good memories directly. When we have to go through the horror of the loss to access anything else, everything else may be experienced as trauma. Trauma makes a shrine of the stuck points, rather than of what deserves remembering. EMDR therapy can remove obstacles and open the possibility of productive grieving.

For a while, we had people who shared our lives. They taught us important things about ourselves and the world. Grief work should clear the way for us to eventually access the good memories, if they exist, without having to first go through the stuck points and the gut punch of the loss. Getting access to the small, important, and meaningful memories is the only tribute that many of us can carry with any kind of ease.

Chapter 46
Additional Strategies for Working With Absences in Memory

There are many reasons why memories or parts of memories might not be accessible. Parts of ourselves may be protecting us from them. Or, they may have occurred during developmental eras in early childhood where discrete autobiographical memories are typically not accessible, yet remnants are held in the body or show up behaviorally. The chapter following this one identifies strategies to find individual memories from developmental eras where trauma was daily, thus no individual ones stand out.

This chapter contains many of the perspectives and strategies that I have found most helpful in working with absences in memory. It is also helpful to consult other EMDR therapists who have worked for decades in these territories (Paulsen, S. and O'Shea, K., 2017).

Respect the Reasons for the Absence

There are many reasons why memories may be absent. If the memory isn't from early childhood, I want to be respectful that the client's system probably has compelling reasons for why the memory isn't accessible to client right now. Being respectful does not mean that I communicate fear to the client. When appropriate, I communicate what I know to be true about the absence: That whatever happened is already over and the costs of it are already being carried by the client's nervous system. Dissociating from memory does not remove all of the tax that the experience had on the nervous system.

When the reason was substance use impairment at the time of the trauma, I'm careful to explain that many substances disrupt normal memory formation, but imprints of the experience are often left even in the absence of concrete memories. We will work to process the parts of the experience that are present, even if those parts show up as the substance is wearing off. We can work on any imprints that the experience made on the client's nervous system by processing on the channels that the client does have.

Work With What You Have First

A very sensible piece of guidance when working with clients with complex trauma who have absences of memory content is to work first and comprehensively with what you do have. The skills, insights, and recovery capital that occur when starting with memory content that is accessible is often essential to working effectively later with voids in memory. Working with absences is next-level EMDR therapy practice and the therapist and the client need to get as prepared as possible for doing this work. Work with what you have first. Then, work with what you have when you are working with memory absences.

When the Void of Memory Is Broad, Explore Where the Boundaries Are

Clients will sometimes come to sessions and report, "I remember nothing before I was 17 years old." When this occurs, I am careful to explore what that means. I may ask the following questions:

- Do you remember where you went to middle school? High school?
- Did you play a sport in high school?
- Did you have friends in high school? Date in high school?
- Do you remember who you lived with when you were in high school? Was it a house or an apartment?
- What is the first clear memory that you have?

I ask these questions to understand the severity, domains, and functional impacts of the absences. Many clients report that they remember nothing before a specific age, yet what they mean is that they have very little day-to-day memory from that era. Others, fortunately not most, have no memory of anything. In cases of profound memory loss, it is important to explore possible organic sources that may account for this loss, including neurological/vascular incidents, periods of heavy drug use, or traumatic brain injury. How I work with a client who does not remember fine details from developmental eras is different from how I work with a client who remembers nothing from entire developmental eras. In cases of profound memory losses after adolescence that are not accounted for by neurological incidents, I assume that the client parts holding those memories are not present or accessible to the parts that are currently in session with me. In these cases, I'm not starting with EMDR therapy. I'm starting with parts work.

Work Backward From Right Now

Many clients who report memory deficits in prior developmental eras often present with intact memory from the past few days, months, or years. Start there. I have found that working in the present and slowly moving back in the timeline is an excellent strategy that allows memory content to appear at rates tolerable to the client's system. Client parts see the progress that the client is making around present-prong targets and make additional content available to awareness as it feels safe to do so. Like a car that is backing up on a road, the more you back up the more of the road that is immediately behind you appears in the rearview mirror. Backing up does not create the road; it simply makes it visible from where you currently are.

You Don't Need to Remember in Order to Heal

It is helpful to remind clients that difficult experiences impact the nervous system in many ways and that it is common for some memories to contain blanks, voids, or missing pieces. Very often, processing the parts of the experience that are present is helpful in resolving the entire experience, including the missing parts of the memory. Again, start with what is present. Often that causes the memory content that is accessible to expand in ways that are helpful for the system to also process the absences.

The Client Demanding That Memory Content Show Up Will Cause Problems

One of the most challenging aspects of working with clients who have only part of a memory is that they get frustrated when the missing pieces of it don't show up on demand. In general, missing pieces of memory content are highly unlikely to appear because the client wants them to. That frustration often comes from the client's assumption that if they cannot remember the content, they cannot heal from it. Endlessly noticing the frustration is a goose chase in EMDR therapy. Try to get ahead of it the moment frustration at voids in memory appears. It is helpful to remind the client that they do not need to remember in order to heal. We can ask questions like: "When you think about the part of the memory that is missing, what are you noticing in your body?" Processing any somatic imprints is an effective way of working with missing narrative or sensory elements of the memory.

The Therapist Must Not Fill in Client Voids

It is essential that therapists do not attempt to fill in any voids in the client's memory. You do not know what happened. Trauma therapists must be careful about suggesting that something specific happened. Never say things like, "I only see responses like this in cases of childhood sexual abuse, etc." We can process a lot of the imprint of what happened without knowing exactly who the abuser was and precisely what they did.

Float the Void Forward to an Early Memory That Exists

When working with preverbal trauma, I want to work with many memories inside EMDR therapy that the client does have access to first. This helps build the skills, resources, and adaptive information needed to successfully work on the bad void. I assume that there will likely be something to target when the client thinks about the void. However, before targeting it directly, I want to see what it floats forward to. Problems show up clinically because they are showing up somewhere in the client's life. Explore what those moments of resonance or reexperiencing are and attempt to process them. For instance, when working with a client who believed that something bad happened to her in very early childhood, I asked: "When you think for just a moment about the bad early experience that you don't remember, what are you noticing in your body? What is the first time that you have a clear memory of your body feeling exactly this way?"

The client reported, "When I was about seven years old, I was sitting at the table at my grandmother's house and one of my older cousins came running down the stairs into the kitchen. I lost my mind. I started screaming." We processed that memory successfully without attempting to make sense of the content of the void directly, although this memory was probably an intrusive re-experiencing of it. Targeting forward gets us into the parts of the brain where parts of the void are stored. It allows us to work on it through proxy before we work void directly. For many of my clients this has been a productive way to work.

With another client, we did the same float forward inquiry, and the client reported: "When I was 14 and dating my first boyfriend, he touched me in a certain way. My response scared both of us." We reprocessed that memory, and it was helpful. I inquired if things like this show up in her current intimate relationships, and we did some future template work around those targets.

Target the Somatics of the Void Directly

Before long, it is important to try to process a preverbal or other void in memory directly. I ask permission from all parts in order to start this work. The language that I use to start the process is a significantly abbreviated Phase Three: "When you think for just a moment about the bad early experience that you don't remember, what are you noticing in your body?" I ask about cognitions, get a VOC, explore emotions, and ask for the SUDs. I ask the client to simply notice whatever is coming on the body channel and proceed into Phase Four to continue with standard protocol.

Do Abundant Future Templates

Memory absences that show up as presenting issues in therapy are doing so because they are showing up somewhere in the client's life. They may also show up in present and future functioning. It is helpful to explore future scenarios connected to the absence. Working effectively with future templates can help resolve problematic behaviors, responses, or avoidance patterns that may impact future functioning.

Chapter 47
Trouble Finding an Individual Memory When Trauma Was Daily

It is usually best to work with an individual memory in EMDR therapy when possible. However, clients with complex trauma will often struggle to identify an individual representative memory when trauma was daily. Many of our floatback approaches are too broad to return anything specific enough to be useful. Floatbacks on cognitions alone may be too broad when there are tens of thousands of memories. They may also struggle with "first" or "worst" when they are attempting to sort a massive dataset of memories. Imagining doing a Google search for: Ohio pizza. That general search returns millions of web pages, nearly all of which are not what we are looking for. Now imagine if we can bring more details to the search and Google Pizza Murray Hill Road Cleveland. That search returns two restaurants that you can eat at today if you live near the Cleveland area. I describe the approach below as a topographic approach to memory selection. Trauma is stored in ways that are "searchable" using body sensations, beliefs about ourselves, the developmental era that the memory occurred, details of who is in the memory (i.e. memories that happened with my "brother," "mother," or "father"), or details of the category of wounding (i.e. sexual abuse, being embarrassed by a parent, or being left out). Memories also happened in spaces, and the topography of those spaces is often encoded into the memory. When our usual strategies to recruit representative memories fail, you can use the following questions to get at a representative memory directly relevant to the present complaint. As you will notice, we do not ask for a specific memory until the end of the process.

The example below is developed when the client reports many present triggers around the cognition "What I want doesn't matter," but the client has struggled to float that cognition back to a single individual memory.

Therapist: "Can you get in touch with that recent memory when your partner ignored your suggestion about dinner plans, and it brought up

'What I want doesn't matter'... What are you noticing in your body right now?"

Client: "I feel like I'm deflating, like a ball that is losing air."

Therapist: "From the point of view of 'What I want doesn't matter' and that deflating feeling, what age (approximately) does that come from? Don't think about a memory, just listen to your gut sense. What age?"

Client: "About eight years old."

Therapist: "Okay, eight years old is about third grade. Check your gut, third grade, 'What I want doesn't matter,' and that feeling, where do you need to work: at home, at school, or in the community?"

Client: "At home."

Therapist: "Can you get a floor plan of the home at the time in your mind? Don't think about individual memories, just check your gut sense using: third grade, 'What I want doesn't matter,' and that body feeling… What room in that home do you associate with those things?"

Client: "The kitchen."

Therapist: "Where in the kitchen?"

Client: "The table."

Therapist: "Which chair at the table?"

Client: "The back left one."

Therapist: "Ok, from the perspective of that chair at that table, 'What I want doesn't matter,' in third grade… put yourself in that chair and look around and let me know the first memory that comes into your awareness."
Client: [pause] "I've got it. It's a memory of my mother giving the last piece of lasagna to my brother and it was my birthday."

Therapist: "Good." [therapist resumes the beginning of Phase Three].

The general structure of this approach is:

1) Identify the negative cognition and recent incident that you would like to float back.
2) Lightly activate the recent incident to get a body feel.
3) Float back the negative cognition and the body feel to an approximate age.
4) Inquire about the context: Home, school, or community.
5) Bring up a floor plan or mental picture of the house, school, or community location and inquire about where (room, etc.) in that space their attention is drawn.
6) Be more specific about where in the room or space (specific chair or place in the space).
7) Put the cognition, age, and the specific place in the space together and target the memory that emerges.

In the vast majority of cases, the memory that emerges will be a representative that helps improve current triggering once processed. Don't forget to work in the future prong with this memory territory as soon as that makes sense.

Phase Eight

"Recovery can take place only within the context of relationships; it cannot occur in isolation. In renewed connections with other people, the survivor recreates the psychological faculties that were damaged or deformed by the traumatic experience."

--Judith Herman, *Trauma and Recovery*

Chapter 48
The Elegance of the Future Prong

It is easy for therapists to be overwhelmed by the sheer volume of past trauma in clients with complex trauma that they may neglect one of the most helpful parts of EMDR therapy: working in the future. Many of our clients have unmanageable lives. This means that they are likely to have an unmanageable next week. Future templates leverage past work, often without taking much session time or the client reporting substantial distress, to help the client visualize, experience, and navigate a future scene more effectively. Future templates create instances of learning for subsequent experiences to connect into. We heal when we have disconfirming experiences. Trauma therapists appreciate that those experiences can be imaginary. Much of what is transformational when working with obsessions, compulsions, and ongoing relationship triggers occurs when working in the future prong.

When We Try the Future Prong Too Soon

If the future template immediately becomes overwhelming to the client, that may be a strong indicator that more work needs to be done in the past before a future template is likely to be successful. If is difficult to predict how much past territory with many clients with complex trauma will need to be resolved before a future template can be completed. Unless there are clear indications that the client is not prepared for a future template, I often invite the client to try it.

The two cases that follow are examples where I advised the client to try to conduct a future template before the client resolved enough of the past content.

> The client, in her early 30s, experienced multiple sexual traumas across multiple different foster placements throughout childhood. The client is currently married to someone who is "safe," and she wanted the moments of sexual intimacy with her husband to be less triggering. The

client was able to resolve multiple memories not connected to sexual abuse prior to working in this area. The client resolved one sexual abuse memory from early childhood across several sessions, but the future template was stopped when the client had flashback-like experiences from the events that she did not resolve in EMDR therapy. We returned to process additional childhood sexual abuse memories, and after resolving multiple memories from other foster placements, the client spontaneously reported that sex with her husband was less triggering. We retried the future template, and it was successful. The client reported substantial improvement in this goal in subsequent sessions.

A client in her late 20s reports that much of her life's wounding is in the theme "what I want doesn't matter" in relation to her mother. The client sometimes depends on her mother financially but also took many steps to distance herself from her mother in other ways during and after college. After working in EMDR therapy around assorted topics, including several memories with her mother around the "what I want doesn't matter" theme, the client reported a wave of anxiety around an upcoming vacation with her boyfriend, her infant child, and her mother. Her mother expressed an intention to babysit her baby during the vacation, and the client was worried that her mother wouldn't respect her dietary restrictions for the infant. The future template was unsuccessful, as we were not able to complete it before the vacation occurred. The client was eventually able to do more past work with this theme and reported that she was able to more comfortably set and defend boundaries with her mother related to herself and her child.

When the future template does not go well, that is not a failure. It is information. Fortunately, struggles in the future template consistently point to the need to do more comprehensive work in the past or to do additional frontloading to address any informational deficits.

General Notes About the Future Prong

Unless something catastrophic is probable, the future template should not be catastrophic. It should target something that is likely to happen in the next few weeks or months. The future template should not be "Let's imagine that your other child also gets hit by a car" or "Can you imagine the scene where your new husband also has a heart attack and dies."

Chapter 49
What Healing Doesn't Give You

Healing will give you a lot that is good. It will help you reset the past. It will let you experience the past as something that is objectively over. It may help your immune system settle. Healing settles a lot of the old tax that you have had to pay to wake up each day in this world. It can give ease back to your breath and unheavy your chest. It can give you some hope. You might find that you wake up on a random Thursday and find it easier to believe that you can find a place here. Resolving memories does not give you the experience of getting your needs met. It helps prepare you for it, but resolving memories does not give you the experience of secure attachment. EMDR therapy does not give you the things that you have to go out into the world to get. Healing prepares you to put new things at risk, and little that is good comes without some real risk and vulnerability.

As you are doing the hard work of recovery, you have to figure out how to interact with yourself, others, and life in completely new ways. You have to learn how to push through the "boredom" of secure attachment when you have spent decades attached to drama. You have to learn how to set and defend boundaries by setting and defending boundaries. You have to learn how to grieve by letting yourself go there. Healing clears your throat for the words "No" and "Yes," but you are the one who has to learn to say them with your own voice and mind.

Phase Eight, in the broadest sense, is also a place where our clients with severe trauma are merging back into the full flow of life. While they may be in their 30s, 40s, 50s, or 60s, they may need continued assistance because they carry legacy deficits into the present despite having done a lot of healing. They are learning how to do things that their non-traumatized peers learned at developmentally appropriate times decades ago. Trauma work with clients with complex trauma is more than simply treating their trauma and discharging them for having met their goals. It's helping them launch in ways that are sustainable. It's helping their new unmortgaged nervous systems have experiences that help clarify who they are, what they are worth, and how they deserve to be treated. It's helping them create new identities and ways of being with themselves, others, and the world.

Short Answers to Common Consult Questions

Chapter 50
Initial Topics

This Is a High-Risk Client

If the client is high-risk, proceed slowly with EMDR therapy reprocessing phases. However, clients with complex trauma also need to heal. Many clients with severe trauma may not become more stable until they do some trauma work. It is generally not a good idea to work intensely in EMDR therapy with a client who is at high risk of decompensating. Clients who are already struggling need supportive care. The higher the risk the client is, the more likely I am to start Flash with them around the issues most contributing most to current distress. When practiced well, Flash is associated with a very low risk of promoting client decompensation.

I'm Overwhelmed by the Volume of the Client's Trauma

It is easy for therapists to be overwhelmed by the volume and complexity of a client's wounding. However, the best strategy is to prepare the client to start working somewhere. One of the biggest risks is that we never start. When the client is prepared to start somewhere, see Chapter 34: Oh My, Where Do We Start? There is no single ideal place to start; just make sure that it is at the intersection of what is productive and what is tolerable. Clients with the most trauma are likely to struggle in Phase Two, so there may be time for clarity in the clinical picture to emerge.

The Client Appears to Have a Profound Lack of Insight

If you are detecting a significant lack of insight, then you are listening closely for the presence of adaptive information. This is excellent. What is the nature of the deficit or misunderstanding and is it central to metabolizing the stuck information that the client is likely to need to work on? Clients who have profound deficits related to human needs may also lack a lot of the adaptive information that may be required to do EMDR therapy well. Part of your Phase Two will need to focus on developing the needed adaptive information. We are always connecting stuck information to adaptive information in EMDR therapy, and this work assumes that the client already has enough adaptive information needed to resolve the stuck information. If this is not the case, it is your job to help the client develop the needed information. You may need to do this through attachment figure resources, parts work, perspective-taking exercises, working on smaller but adjacent targets in EMDR therapy, or other experiential techniques.

The Client Appears Emotionally Dead

Clients need to be emotionally online to do the EMDR processing phases well. They should be embodied enough to notice. See Chapter 13: Phase Two Isn't Just Mindfulness Resources for some suggestions.

The Client Is Always Profoundly Dysregulated

EMDR therapy reprocessing is typically a dive into distress. Clients need to have the capacity to feel worse on any given day that reprocessing occurs. However, I have worked with many clients who have a baseline level of 8/10 stress or distress, and they can do EMDR therapy well once adequately prepared and using strategies described in Chapter 37: How We Interact With the Memory Matters and Chapter 38: The Videotape Approach.

Processing Goes Well, But Client Reports Instability After Sessions

We have to work differently if EMDR therapy is causing significant client instability between sessions. If the client is unable to function, reports debilitating memory flooding, or increases in high-risk behaviors or thoughts, it is important to make some changes before proceeding. Here are some suggestions:

- Difficulties between sessions can indicate that embers were spread during the client's session that caught fire in the hours and days after reprocessing. Explore this. Is the distressing content that is coming up from the same developmental era where we were working? If so, we need to incorporate into closure the anticipation that this will happen again and send the client home with a concrete (and possibly written) plan to better manage this. If it continues to happen, this may be an indicator that they are simply working in too nested or complex of a territory for right now. Again, it is advisable to work in territories that are productive and tolerable. If a memory territory is causing intolerable responses after the session, then that isn't a tolerable territory, or the client needs specific enhanced resources to manage what is emerging. Shift to a territory that is more tolerable.

- If the difficulty emerges after working on an attachment wound memory, did you end the session with their attachment figure resource? If you are working on attachment wounds, it is important to end the session with their attachment figure resource to prevent attachment embers from spreading after the session. Using a well-developed and well-practiced attachment figure resource generally ends the multi-day difficulties that often occur following attachment work.
- If the client's decompensation is from a single childhood memory that emerged but was not processed in that EMDR session, you may need to pivot to the memory that is causing distress in either EMDR therapy or Flash to try to resolve it.

The Client Is Worried That EMDR Will Surface Forgotten Memories

Rarely does EMDR therapy processing unexpectedly surface completely dissociated memory content that no part of the client knew existed. However, this client's worry isn't coming from nowhere, and the worry isn't limited to doing EMDR therapy. It is helpful to explore why this worry exists, what makes the client suspect that dissociated memory exists, and why the client thinks it is likely to emerge in EMDR therapy. Many media treatments of EMDR therapy in popular television series that clients may have been exposed to depict EMDR as a way to surface repressed memories.

It is essential that therapists do not attempt to fill in any blanks in memory. This is a matter of ethics and sound clinical practice. Clients do not need to remember in order to heal in EMDR therapy. However, if they do remember, that can help make their healing less complicated. It can also be helpful for the client to understand that if repressed memories do emerge, we will be able to effectively target them the same way that we do any other memories. We want to normalize the client's worries about the emergence of new information. We want to be sensitive to the reality that the information contained in these memories could potentially have disrupting implications for the client's family system (this is often a client worry). It is also helpful to let the client know that whatever has happened to the client (whether they remember it or not), the nervous system is already carrying the weight of it and has been paying the tax on it. It is already seeping out into different parts of the self and different aspects of functioning.

When appropriate, I will sometimes communicate something like the following:

> If something bad happened to you that you don't remember, I hope that some part of you can appreciate what I know for sure about it: that whatever happened is already over. It is not happening right now. If something does emerge, we can work on it and resolve it. We can use multiple different strategies to do that. I would like to start working on what you do have before we try to work on absences, but I'm committed to doing this work with you.

Also, see Chapter 46: Additional Strategies for Working With Absences.

Clients With Borderline Tendencies

Clients with Borderline tendencies will often struggle with many of the core tasks of EMDR therapy. They often struggle with self-regulation, often have poor somatic awareness of distress until it comes in intolerable volumes, and have strong insecurities around "how do I know that the people who are there for me are there for me?" Clients with Borderline tendencies may need enhanced EMDR resourcing related to emotional regulation. Inconsistent childhood attachment is often a key component, and this type of wounding often shows up in EMDR therapy as profound deficits in adaptive information related to human needs. With adequate preparation and good front-loading, clients with Borderline tendencies can do good work in EMDR therapy, but this work is often a slow and challenging process. It may require regular intervention to keep the client on track. If clients with Borderline tendencies really need to heal but are struggling in EMDR therapy, they do tend to thrive with Flash approaches around whatever is getting stuck in EMDR or whatever is causing present dysregulation. Flash approaches around future targets after clearing past ones are particularly helpful with this population. Flash can be an effective bridge to support stability for subsequent EMDR work.

The Client Reports a History of Unresponsive Episodes

This is a very broad territory. Try to understand as much about the shutdown response as possible, including what (if anything) triggers it, how long it usually lasts, what happens during it, what (if any) assistance the client needs during it, and what helps the client get out of it. If the client has psychogenic seizures or other processes that render the client unable to respond or exercise agency, have a concrete plan in place with the client about what the client needs you to do and who you will contact (make sure that you have appropriate signed releases already in place in the event of client incapacitation to make this even less stressful or risky). Of course, it is important to work in tolerable areas in EMDR therapy and help make sure that the client is staying well within their window of tolerance. If the client is having intrusive symptoms and is not adequately prepared to do trauma work or does not have the current window of tolerance needed, Flash (particularly the Four Blinks version) is an appropriate intervention since care is taken at every step to make sure distress is being routed away from the client's nervous system.

When Clients Report Prior Harm From EMDR Therapy

EMDR therapy is popular enough for a lot of therapists to be conducting it poorly. Even when therapists do practice EMDR therapy well and ethically, clients can still be harmed. It is helpful to try to understand what occurred in the prior EMDR session that was overwhelming or caused the difficulty and work to explore a range of alternatives. Sometimes, the client's prior EMDR therapy is stored as trauma. There are times when we cannot use EMDR therapy to resolve the harm that EMDR caused them. You may need to work in other approaches first (such as Flash) to resolve EMDR-related injury before using EMDR as a therapeutic intervention.

Rethinking Marijuana and Benzo Use

Cautions abound in the EMDR community related to client marijuana and benzo use. However, I don't believe that a client has ever been harmed by attempting EMDR therapy with recent use of either. It is true that both *might* prevent activation. Preventing or significantly impairing activation ensures that the client's EMDR session isn't going to go anywhere, but it also isn't likely to cause the client harm. Try it. If the client struggles to effectively activate, plan subsequent sessions as far away as possible from the last use. These substances are ubiquitous with clients with complex trauma, and both are commonly prescribed by licensed practitioners other than myself. I have no business telling a client when to take or not take a prescribed substance. There are so many things that might cause harm inside EMDR therapy, marijuana and benzodiazepine use are not likely to be among them.

Chapter 51
Phase One Topics

How Much Client History Is Advisable?

See the section of this book labeled Phase One. Clients with complex trauma will confound your attempts to overly organize their recovery. It is generally a bad idea to do an extensive and detailed trauma history the first time you meet someone or months before the client begins their first target. You do not need all of this information in order to effectively start somewhere at the intersection of what is productive and tolerable. Consider these questions. How much client history would be productive and tolerable with this client right now? Are there other, more important clinical tasks? What am I going to do in the next few weeks with a large amount of information related to past trauma for this client? Are there risks in opening up more information than we have the time and ability to work on today? Do you need to know today? Are you sure?

Chapter 52
Phase Two Topics

The Client Struggles to Visualize

Many thousands of people have presented to EMDR therapists with difficulties visualizing things and have not been able to engage in EMDR therapy because so many of the standard EMDR resources are visualization focused. See Part Two of the book, especially the sections on Dip Your Toe in resources. Outsource the visualization components of the resource to a YouTube video. There is no compelling reason why the resource needs to be imaginary.

The Client Struggles to Emotionally Connect to a Resource

Struggling to connect to some resources can be an indicator of somatic disconnection, but this depends on the resource. The container resource is a box to hold stuff. We might not expect someone to have a deep emotional response to a box. The goal in using the resource is to successfully create it as a mental construct so that we can subsequently use it when needed. The client reporting no shift in affective state in the calm scene or other resources where the shift in affect is the point of the resource should be noted and explored. Again, problems in Phase Two are canaries in the coal mine for EMDR therapy reprocessing phases.

How to Know When the Client Is Prepared Enough to Start Somewhere

There may be plenty of indicators that the client is not prepared. It's hard to know for sure when the client is prepared enough to start somewhere. See Chapter 31: What Does Prepared Enough Mean?

Chapter 53
Phase Three through Seven Topics

The Client Doesn't Want to Return to a Partially Resolved Memory

Clients experience EMDR therapy differently than we do. A memory that was an 8/10 and is now a 3/10 isn't likely causing the client any right-now problems. It will feel, from their perspective, that they have much more pressing issues to resolve than that remaining 3/10. They aren't wrong. However, really good things happen when memories fully and adaptively resolve in EMDR therapy, and we need those good things for future targets. It is okay to have some memories "open" in EMDR therapy (in fact, complex trauma will pretty much guarantee that sometimes), but it is also important that we close them. On any given day, the client's goal may be simply to feel better. Our broader goal is to help the client reset his nervous system.

How Bad Is It for the Client to Have "Open" Targets

An open target is an unresolved memory, but the term is a bit misleading. While it is possible for EMDR therapy to contribute to the client opening a lot of memory territory that might result in the client destabilizing between sessions, simply having unresolved memory targets is rarely a contributor to that. Overactivation and working in intolerable territories might. Many new EMDR therapy trainees speak about unresolved memory targets in ways similar to an open wound. When we activate a tolerable memory in EMDR therapy and work in sensible ways, it is in working memory for a few hours until the nervous system returns the unprocessed parts to where trauma is stored in the brain. This does not mean that clients won't feel resonance, exhaustion, or adjacent memory activation days after EMDR therapy. The aftermath of EMDR reprocessing is something that we always want to inquire about, and when the client is struggling between sessions, we may need to shift how or where we are working. If the client is away from therapy for a few weeks, unresolved memories aren't generally the liability that many new EMDR therapists seem to think they are. The nervous system knows what to do with the debris. It has been carrying it for decades probably. Also see Chapter 44: Why Finishing Things Matters in EMDR Therapy for a more detailed exploration.

The Client Did Great EMDR, Now They Don't Want to Resume It

This is the most sensible thing in the universe that confuses many new EMDR therapists. You just witnessed a client resolve a memory. They report astonishment. They did not know that they could heal from anything so quickly. You may think that they will return next session and want to work on a new memory. They probably will not. Why? Because they have experienced conflicting things in EMDR therapy. They have experienced healing. They also experienced that EMDR therapy is really difficult. It requires that they sit for long periods noticing the very things that they have spent their lives trying not to feel. The client can come to a talk therapy session and feel heard and validated. They get a predictable benefit from that. They can come to an EMDR session, and they cannot accurately predict how much it will suck. It's a gamble, and the benefit is at least partially unknowable. When you notice this dynamic, explore it with the client. Remind the client that we can work in more tolerable memory territories and that we have options in how we interact with the memory.

The Client Has an Issue to Work On, But No Individual Memory Emerges

Is the client struggling to identify a specific relevant memory because childhood trauma was daily and no individual memories stand out? See Chapter 47: Trouble Finding an Individual Memory when Trauma Was Daily. When first starting, it is wise to start with recent occurrences of the trouble or problem. It is also easier for many clients to find more recent instances of difficulties.

Lots of Memories Are Showing Up in Reprocessing

Very little good will come with clients with pervasively complex trauma when lots of memories want to come. We need memory content to come, but we need it to come at a tolerable and digestible rate and intensity. See

Chapter 40: When to Let New Memories In, When to Container for concrete guidance when memories want to flood in.

The Client Activates and Then Quickly Shuts Down

An immediate or almost immediate shutdown response at the beginning of Phase Four generally comes from one of these sources (or a combination):

- The client is attempting to work in memory territory that is not currently tolerable to the client. See Chapter 35 Oh My, Where Do We Start.
- One or more of the client's parts does not consent to working in this territory. See Chapter 26: More About Consent from Parts.
- Memory content came into awareness at a rate faster than the client had the capacity to notice and digest and immediately pushed the client out of his window of tolerance. See Chapter 37: How We Interact With the Memory Matters for options that may allow distress to come into awareness in more tolerable pieces.
- This is the first attempt at an attachment wound target and it is simply bigger than the adaptive information that the client has accessible. See Chapter 42: The Quicksand of Attachment Wound Targets.

Chapter 29: And Then the Client Dissociated can also be helpful in these cases.

The Client Does Not Activate

If the client activates and then shuts down, see the topic above. If the client fails to activate across multiple targets, are you sure that the client is embodied enough to notice? EMDR therapy is a somatic psychotherapy and activation often requires some level of embodiment. See Chapter 13: Phase Two Isn't Just Mindfulness Resources. When appropriate, see the topic above related to recent marijuana and benzo use.

The Client Only Tells Me Thoughts

If the client appears to be trying to figure out the memory or appears to be processing on the thought channel without any noticing, I am likely to stop them. These strategies are often bypasses around the distress I'm asking them to activate and notice. See Chapter 34: There is Nothing to Figure Out Today.

We Have Tried to Process This Memory for Many Sessions

Sometimes, we simply need to process a target even if it takes multiple sessions. However, in these cases, I can articulate a clear reason why this makes clinical sense. Here are some of the reasons why I may recommend that we stick with a difficult memory across multiple sessions:

- It is presenting as a Mount Everest that is blocking or obscuring everything else. This is frequently the case with child loss, relationship betrayal, existential health crises, or related. There isn't going to be another target that is accessible.
- We have worked on many memories successfully and this is our first major attachment wound memory. Attachment wound memories often take multiple sessions when we first encounter them. I always make sure that we end them with adequate attachment figure resources to put out any embers that this work may spread.
- The client struggled with this memory but made good progress with it. The trajectory is good, and the client had a tolerable experience after the prior session ended.
- The client struggled with this memory, and it did not seem to shift much from my perspective, but the client indicated that she would like to keep working on it and that things are shifting for her in helpful ways.

Other than the above reasons, I'm unlikely to recommend a second session resuming work on a memory that did not shift at all or caused a hard shutdown response. When my clients with complex trauma are attached to whales or nuclear-powered submarines, I suggest that we get scissors and disconnect from them as soon as it becomes clear that the target is larger than what is tolerable today.

Continually attempting to target a single memory without any real progress or movement is a risky activity with clients with complex trauma. If you feel the compulsion to continue to return to an intolerable and unproductive target, consider these questions:

- Is there a solid clinical reason why this is the hill that you want the client to die on?
- If we are connecting stuck information to adaptive information, do you suspect that there is enough adaptive information for this memory to connect to and metabolize into? What is the evidence of that? See Chapter 36: The Canaries in the Coal Mine.

The Client Is Struggling to Stay Regulated in Phase Four

Consider if one or more of these scenarios seem to describe the client's struggle:

- Is it possible that this memory turned out to be bigger than the client anticipated? In fact, is it bigger than the client's boat of adaptive information? If so, you can always disconnect from it and go to Phase Seven and work in more tolerable memory territories.
- Is the client opening up a lot of adjacent memory content? Try to keep them focused on this memory. See Chapter 40: When to Let New Memories In, When to Container.
- Does the client seem to be pushing into the memory rather than taking a bite of it and noticing deeply that bite? You can always encourage the client to notice what is happening in their body during the BLS and invite the client not to think about the bad memory during the BLS. You can always send them back to the target when the current channel of distress starts to dissipate.
- Back to the EMDR therapy Tricycle metaphor, EMDR therapy reprocessing involves three primary components: tolerable activation, noticing, and BLS. Is the client stuck doing something other than one of those three things? Are they trying to figure out something? Are they actively noticing? Are they stuck in guilt, shame, blame, responsibility? If so, Chapter 41: Where Clients Get Stuck and How to Intervene is likely to be helpful.

Dissociative Processes are Showing Up

Dissociation is often a byproduct of overactivation. See Chapter 29: And Then the Client Dissociated, for strategies to help the client stay grounded enough to work effectively, depending on how dissociation is showing up in the client's session.

The Client is Walking Through the Memory Step by Step, But Not Noticing

Many clients assume that this is what EMDR therapy requires. That is how we do other therapies that they may have done or heard about. They are missing the central component: noticing. With clients with severe trauma, I do not want them to walk through the memory from beginning to end. I want them to engage with the memory briefly and then notice deeply what comes from that "bite." Slow down, take a bite, and notice, notice, notice. That's how we do EMDR therapy well with clients with complex trauma. EMDR therapy is different from our regular approach to problems. It is different from what we have done in prior therapy. We are doing EMDR therapy now because it is different, therefore our doing of it should not revert to our old ineffective strategies.

The SUDs Will Not Go Lower than a One, Two, or Three

While your Phase Four scripts may not capture this nuance, the SUDs is an evaluation of the amount of distress that remains in the memory that you started Phase Three with only. It does not matter that you have had a lot of similar wounds in your life. Those other memories aren't our right-now target. It does not matter, from the point of view of the SUDs, that your mother continues to do these things to you. We can work on that with a future template. From the point of view of the SUDs, it does not matter that the negative cognition still feels true for you in your right-now life and the positive cognition does not feel true for you. These are not the questions that constitute the SUDs. We are in Phase Four and for the purposes of Phase Four, I want you to put a 100-foot brick wall at the beginning of that memory and another 100-foot brick wall at the end of that memory. Between those two walls only, how much distress is in that memory? If it's not a zero, what is it that keeps it from being a zero? Identify it and have the client name it. When they find it, notice it. When they do notice it, 99% of the time it goes lower. It does not matter that the client says that the distress isn't going to go any lower than a one, two, or three that it currently is. It was just a seven and the client didn't think it would go lower than seven. Identify it and notice it, and it is very, very likely to go lower.

Problems with Installation

Phase Five is largely cleaning up debris on the thought channel from the core of the work that was done in Phase Four. In the vast majority of sessions, more than 90% of the desensitization and reprocessing is done in Phase Four. Like with the SUDs, it is important that you realize that the VOC is an evaluation of how true the positive belief feels right now related to the memory that you started Phase Three with only. Because there is so much redundant trauma learning with people with complex trauma, the client can come to believe something positive about themselves fully related to a single memory, yet not believe the same positive thing at all more broadly. This is completely normal for complex trauma. If Phase Five is becoming more complicated than this summary suggests, then it is likely because of one of these reasons (and most of them are easily fixable):

- The client is rating the VOC of the positive cognition based on how they feel about themselves generally right now, rather than related to how true it feels related to the target memory from Phase Three only. Clarify that the VOC is related to the target memory only. What specifically in that memory makes that positive belief not 7/7 true? Identify that. Notice that deeply. Again, it does not matter that the positive cognition does not hold more broadly. That's not what we are evaluating.
- While you probably did check to see if the positive cognition changed when you first moved into Phase Five, sometimes the problem with installing the positive cognition is that you are trying to install the wrong belief. If the cognition that the client is trying to install doesn't seem like it fits, ask the client: "What is easier to believe about yourself related to the memory that we started with right now?" Install that cognition.
- Other memories may have made their way into working memory and the client may not have told you. Transitioning from Phase Four to Phase Five is often a time when other memories want to come. When distress comes unexpectedly in Phase Five, check to make sure that new memory content has not emerged without your

awareness. If so, container it. Attempt to resume Phase Five if there is time. If not, pivot to closure.

Importantly, Phase Five is an opportunity to slow down and have the disconfirming experience of sitting with a difficult experience and noticing the schema shift. We do not want to rush Phase Five. We have spent all that time noticing distress, so let's be present with the good stuff too. The client has had very little experience sitting with recovery, resilience, redemption, resolution, or peace.

Problems With Body Scan

Phase Six is largely cleaning up debris on the body channel from the core work that was done in Phase Four. The vast majority of the work and difficult noticing occurs in Phase Four. If Phase Six becomes unexpectedly complicated, it may be because of one of these reasons:

- Other memory content not related to the target memory is making its way into working memory. New memories want to come as old ones are wrapping up. Anticipate this and remind the client that the door to awareness is their door and not everything that wants to come into awareness at the end of a session should be allowed to.
- Pain. The client may report sensations when their baseline state of the body is varying degrees of pain. If it is unclear if the pain is from the memory, from an organic body state, or from simply sitting for so long in one position, ask them to get comfortable and notice it.

Phase Six is an opportunity to slow down and have the disconfirming experience of sitting with a previously difficult experience and noticing the positive or neutral body response. We do not want to rush Phase Six. We have spent a lot of time noticing distress, let's be present with the good stuff too. The client has had very little experience sitting with recovery, resilience, redemption, resolution, or peace.

Mindful Closure Strategies Do Not Lower Distress Much

Sometimes, clients become overactivated or pervasively shut down in the processing phases and our attempts to use mindfulness resources in Phase

Seven are largely ineffective. If this is the case, you can try one of the following strategies:

- Ground. Grounding is one of the most powerful resources. It connects the client to the "safety" of the present and may be required before the client can be present enough to engage in the other mindfulness resources that you may have planned for them in Phase Seven.
- Is the client stuck in the existential loneliness of an attachment wound? See Chapter 42: The Quicksand of Attachment Wound Targets. It is best to teach attachment figure resources before you need them. They are very difficult to teach when the client is stuck inside an existentially lonely state activated by a difficult EMDR session.

Chapter 54
Phase Eight Topics

Successfully Discharging Clients

It is not unusual for clients with complex trauma to begin the therapy process with the presenting issue being a specific issue, crisis, or unmanageable trauma symptom. It is great when clients can engage in comprehensive trauma treatment and work until they have largely reset their nervous system. Or, they may work for a while until that presenting issue starts to settle and they may self-discharge or request discharge. It may take a few months or years before the next layers of the onion that is complex trauma start resonating, and they may need to return to therapy. This is relatively common and okay. This was true in my own recovery. I keep discovering new areas where complex trauma caused issues in my internal world, functioning, or relationships. I keep returning to therapy to resolve the next layers of the complex trauma onion and it is the process of living that often surfaces the next layers. Personally, I am not hopeful that I will find the little green sprig at the center of my complex trauma onion. I may never fully meet the self that I long to be, but I am certain that every day I am getting closer. Healing from complex trauma is the work of a lifetime. There are effective strategies, but there are no brief approaches to psychotherapy when wounding is complex.

Frequency of Future Templates

How often should you be doing future templates? As often as you can. I find that most EMDR therapists I consult with do not consider future templates often enough. See Chapter 48: The Elegance of the Future Prong for more guidance.

When Clients Resolve Some Memories but Aren't Getting Dramatically Better

A client with severely complex trauma who is 47 years old has probably occupied a pervasively traumatized nervous system for 400,000 hours. That is a lot of deeply salient learning and reexperiencing. The lessons from that type of learning aren't meant to be shifted with ease. It can take three years of weekly sessions to help many clients with pervasively traumatized nervous systems reset their nervous systems. This assumes that we are doing reprocessing work in many of those sessions.

Here is the good news. If we are seeing a client one hour every week, we are seeing them one hour out of 168 hours in a week. If we are working with them for three years and they are largely able to reset their nervous system in those three years of work, they will have done that in fewer hours than there are in one whole week of their life. Said more clearly, it is possible for a 47-year-old client to process 400,000 hours of difficult existence in less than one week of actual treatment time. That is remarkable. That is an efficient way to work, but it is not brief as defined by insurance companies and other service gatekeepers. Understanding this is key to understanding why clients with complex trauma do not get better immediately or even in the short term. It will allow us to advocate for our clients more effectively. It will help make sure that we are at least dying on the right hill. As EMDR therapists who treat complex trauma, we should stop referring to EMDR therapy as a brief approach to psychotherapy when most trauma globally is of the complex type. We should simply stop it. It confuses clients. It confuses trainees. Brief is the wrong word. It is deceptive, even if it is unintentionally so.

References

Ecker, B., Ticic, R., & Hulley, L. (2024). *Unlocking the emotional brain*. Taylor & Francis.

Marich, J. (2023). *Dissociation made simple*. North Atlantic Books.

Parnell, L. (2013). *Attachment-focused EMDR: Healing relational trauma*. New York: W.W. Norton & Company.

Paulsen, S. & O'Shea, K. (2017). *When there are no words: Repairing early trauma from the attachment period in EMDR therapy*. Createspace.

Schmidt, S. J. (2009). *The developmental needs meeting strategy: An ego state therapy for healing adults with childhood trauma and attachment wounds*. DNMS Institute.

Schwartz, R. C., & Sweezy, M. (2020). *Internal family systems therapy* (2nd ed.). The Guilford Press.

Shapiro, R. (2016). *Easy ego state Interventions: Strategies for working with parts*. W. W. Norton & Company.

Shapiro, F. (2018). *Eye movement desensitization and reprocessing (EMDR) therapy: Basic principles, protocols, and procedures* (3rd ed.). The Guilford Press.

van der Kolk, B. A. (2014). *The body keeps the score: Brain, mind, and body in the healing of trauma*. Viking.

Index

absences of memory, 161-165
accommodations, in Phase Two, 50
activation, problems, 184
adaptive information, assessing for, 123; become less accessible when overactivated, 125-126; client needs enough, 38-39; comes to you, 112; deficits, 93-99; deficits in, 122-126; how to develop, 53-54; in well-resourced clients, 32; isn't one thing, 103; need to assess for, 26-27
anxiety, of the therapist, 17
attachment figure resources, 53-64; are parts work, 53-64, 154-155; assessing for need, 56-58; explaining, 57; homework, 63; modifications, 79; qualities, 58; why develop, 57
attachment wounds, 153-155; assessing for, 28-29; like quicksand, 151-152
avoidance of EMDR, by client, 183

Barn Door metaphor, 108-109
bean bag technique, to titrate activation, 129
benzodiazepine use, rethinking, 178-179
bilateral stimulation, 14
blame, as blocks, 123, 149
blocked processing, 140-150
blocking beliefs, as a Phase Two problem, 93-99
blocks, common, 39
blue smoke breathing resource, 76-77
Boat and the Whale metaphor, 11-13; 128-129
body scan, 72; problems with, 189
Borderline tendencies, 175, 177-178
breathing, 76-78
bridge resources, 50
Bright Yellow Line in Road metaphor, 18, 112
Brownie Mix metaphor, 109

calm scene, modified script, 74; problems, 81-82
Canaries in the Coal Mine metaphor, 122-126
car, cinder block on gas pedal metaphor, 49-50; journey metaphor, 102
catatonic shutdown responses, 178
Cinder Block on Gas Pedal metaphor, 49-50
client isn't getting better, 192
closure strategies, are ineffective, 189
Cognitive Behavioral Therapy, 98
cognitive processing, trying to figure out the memory, 111-112, 149-150, 185
Cognitive Processing Therapy, 98
coherence therapy, 5-7

completing targets, is important, 156-157
complex trauma, assessing for, 28-29; developmental disruptions, 12; ongoing life events, 20
consent from parts, 80, 144
container, problems, 82-83
containment, essential for trauma work, 85-88
conversion shutdowns, 178

decompensation after sessions, 175-176
developmental needs, and blocking beliefs, 95-96
Developmental Needs Meeting Strategy, 44
developmental trauma, 153-155; 166-168
Dialectical Behavioral Therapy, 98
dip your toe in resources, 66-84
discharging clients, 191
disconfirmation, 5-7, 189; 189; and mindfulness, 48-49, 51; parts work, 53-64
dissociated memories, worries about, 176-177
dissociation, 89-92, 178, 184, 187
dysregulated clients, 175
Ecker, Bruce, 5-7

embodiment, need for, 37-38, 46, 103
EMDR, as a brief approach, critique, 21; clients need capacity to feel worse, 20; complex trauma and lots of hats, 20; difficulty slowing down, 19; disconfirming experiences, 6; explaining, 33-35; foundational training and complex trauma, 21; is not a magic wand, 14-15; marketed as an easy intervention, 16; mechanism, 5-6; rigid adherence to protocol, 11; staying out of the way, 13; therapist retention, 10
empathy, between parts is essential, 124
energy, managing, 147
ethics, of not treating trauma, 9-10
existential loneliness, 123-124, 152; 152; see also attachment wounding,
existential questions, are often blocks, 148

feeder memories, 138-139
fire extinguisher resources, 65
first memory, don't start there, 115
Flash, 8, 175, 177, 178
flashbacks, resource for, 70-71
flooding, during reprocessing, 147-148, 183-184, 186
future templates, 165; frequency of, 191

generalization, to other memories, 136-137, 156-157
getting out of the way, 121

Green Sign on the Highway, metaphor, 112
grief, 158-160
Grill in the Backyard metaphor, 137
guilt, as blocks, 123, 149

hand breathing resource,
harm from prior EMDR therapy, 178
healthy clients, well resourced by life, 32
high risk clients, 174
homework, practice at baseline, 51

inadequate preparation, problems from, 143-144
information, comes as a gift, 110-111
informed consent, 100-101; as a Phase Two task, 105-106
insight, client lack of, 174-175
instability after sessions, 175-176
installation problems, 188-189
Internal Family Systems, 44
interweaves, are perspective changes, 142-143

light stream, problems, 84

magic, when there is none, 153
Marathon metaphor, 118
Marich, Jamie, 44
marijuana use, rethinking, 178-179
memory, coming into awareness too quickly, 18
memory absences, 161-165
memory content, other memories want to come, 135-139; putting a fence around the target, 135-136; too much is a block, 148-149
memory losses, 91-92
mindfulness, difficult for clients, 45-52; embodiment, ; is not a machine, 45; present moment, 46
Mount Everest, don't start there, 118-119

noticing, and blocks, 147-148; as the bright yellow line in the EMDR road, 18; being concrete about, 109; challenges with, 46-47; externalizing, 50-51; not noticing, 187
numb, client is emotionally dead, 175

onion of trauma, 3, 191
open targets, 182-183
overactivation, 186; and dissociation, 90-91; is a problem, 125-126

Parnell, Laurel, 55-64
parts work, 154-155; attachment resources, 53-64; central to EMDR, 41-44; consent in all phases, 48, 80; developing adaptive information, 53-64; disconfirming experiences, 7, 54; to develop adaptive information, 97; to manage cognitive agendas, 149-150
performance anxiety, and mindfulness, 47
perspective changes, interventions are perspective changes, 142-143
perspective-taking exercises, 96-97
Phase Eight, 169-172; and the need for more experiential learning, 172; future template, 169-172
Phase Four, interacting with the memory tolerably, 127-130
Phase One, 180; agency settings, 26; assess adaptive information, 11-12; default approaches, 24; need to also assess for adaptive information, 26-27; somatic deficits, 27; with complex trauma, 24-30
Phase Seven, 189
Phase Six, problems with, 189
Phase Three, selecting tolerable targets, 127-130
Phase Two, externalizing noticing, 50-51; more than mindfulness, 32-40; problems with resources, 181; when resourced enough, 100
preparation, meanings of, 100
present awareness, and blocks, 147
present moment, 46; safety in, 36-37
present safety, 101-102
productive and tolerable, 116-117
psychoeducation, about their role, 107

Quicksand metaphor, 151-152

racing mind, and mindfulness, 47
relaxation response, is not primary goal initially, 48-49
Resource Therapy, 44
resources, body scan, 72; flashbacks, 70-71; practice at baseline, 51; sensory grounding, 68-69
responsibility, as blocks, 123, 149
restricted processing, 107-109, 127-130
resuming incomplete targets, 182-183

schema, 5-6
sensory grounding resource, 68-69, 87
shame, as blocks, 123, 149
Shapiro, Robin, 44
shutdown responses, 184
somatic awareness, 27
somatic dissociation, 91

somatic interventions, 7
somatic processing of absences, 165
standard resources, where they go wrong, 81-84
start by starting somewhere, 110-111
stuck processing, 140-150; is the target a memory, 145; what stuck looks like, 141-142
SUDs, will not go lower, 187-188
suicidal clients, 174

target selection, problems when trauma was daily, 166-168; start by starting somewhere, 116; therapist overwhelm, 174; where to start, 113-121
targeting order, working backward with memory absences, 163
targeting problems is the target a memory, 145
targeting the same memory many sessions, 185-186
time, making resources more tolerable by decreasing, 48
titration, 127-130
topographic approach, to finding individual memories, 166-168
touchstone memory, clients who want to start with, 124
trauma, explaining, 33; necessitates survival strategies, 3-4
Tricycle metaphor, 14-15; 90
trying to figure out the trauma, 111-112
Tunnel metaphor, 157

underactivation, 184

Video Game metaphor, 157
videotape approach, 131-134
visualization, problems with, 74, 181
VOC, of one, 122
voids of memory, 161-165; worries about, 176-177

Wagner, Amy, 44
walking through the memory, but not noticing, 187
whales of memory, 145-146
window of tolerance, 146; need to expand, 35-36
worst memory, don't start there, 115

YouTube, in calm scene, 74

www.ingramcontent.com/pod-product-compliance
Lightning Source LLC
Chambersburg PA
CBHW060459030426
42337CB00015B/1644